Madison Julius Cawein

Lyrics and Idyls

Madison Julius Cawein

Lyrics and Idyls

ISBN/EAN: 9783743328785

Manufactured in Europe, USA, Canada, Australia, Japa

Cover: Foto ©ninafisch / pixelio.de

Manufactured and distributed by brebook publishing software
(www.brebook.com)

Madison Julius Cawein

Lyrics and Idyls

LYRICS AND IDYLS

BY

MADISON JULIUS CAWEIN.

TO

James Lane Allen

AND

Robert Burns Wilson,

WITH REGARD AND APPRECIATION FOR THE HIGH STANDARD OF BEAUTY THE EXCELLENCY OF THEIR WORK, PROSE AND POETICAL, HAS GIVEN TO SOUTHERN LITERATURE.

CONTENTS.

WITH HARPE AND PYPE.

IDEAL DIVINATION,	9
THE BEAUTIFUL,	13
OVERSEAS,	16
PORPHYROGENITA,	19
ORIENTAL ROMANCE,	22
LOVE I HAD BANISHED,	24
HE TELLS,	26
SHE SPEAKS,	29
UNCERTAINTY,	31
FALL,	34
BENEATH THE BEECHES,	36
ANDALIA,	38
NOERA,	41
JULIA,	44
LORA,	46
BLANCH,	48
PHYLLIS,	49
VALKYRIEN,	52
MOTHS,	54
AS IT IS,	56
THOUGHTS,	57
AFTER THE TOURNAMENT,	59
AMONG THE ACRES OF THE WOOD,	61
LOVE A-MILKING,	63

CONTENTS.

ROMANTIC LOVE, ... 65
PASTORAL LOVE, ... 68
IMMORTAL, ... 70
SLEEP, ... 72
GHOSTLY WEATHER, ... 75
THE BRIDLE-PATH, ... 76
NOONING, ... 81
THE LOG-BRIDGE, ... 83
THE OLD FARM, ... 86
AMONG THE KNOBS, ... 90
GARGAPHIE, ... 94
ROSICRUCIAN, ... 97
HIS SONG, ... 100
APOCALYPSE, ... 102
ILLUSION, ... 103
DUTY AND LOVE, ... 104

SHAPES AND SHADOWS.

BLODEUWEDD, ... 107
THE LADY OF VERNE, ... 113
THE SUCCUBA, ... 119
HIS FIRST MISTRESS, ... 128
BEFORE THE BALL, ... 131
MASKS, ... 134
HAUNTED, ... 138
UNDER THE GREENWOOD TREE, ... 144
REVISITED, ... 148
LOST LOVE, ... 151
LYANNA, ... 153
GLORAMONE, ... 160
THE CAVERNS OF KAF, ... 168
THE SPIRIT OF THE VAN, ... 176
THE SPIRIT OF THE STAR, ... 182
AT NINEVEH, ... 189
ROMAUNT OF THE OAK, ... 192

With Harpe and Pype.

IDEAL DIVINATION.

How I have thought of her,
  Her I have never seen!—
Now from a raying air
She, like a romance queen,
Flowers a face serene,
Radiant in raven hair.

Now in a balsam scent
Laughs from the stars that gleam;
Naked and redolent,
Bends to me breasts of beam,
Eyes that will make me dream,
Throat that the dimples dent.

Love is all vain to me
So: and as dust severe,
Faith: and a barren tree,
Truth: and a bitter tear,
Joy: for I wait and hear
Her who can never be.

Living we learn to know
Life is not worth its pain;
Living we find a woe
Under each joy we gain;
Fardled of hope we strain
Whither no hope may know.

Life is too credulous
Of Time who beckons on.
Memory still serves us thus—
Gauging the coming dawn
By a day dead and gone,
Day that's a part of us.

Soul—of life's sins so mocked,
Clayed in the flesh and held,
Ever rebellion rocked,

Battling, forever quelled,
Yearning on heaven spelled
Over of stars—lies locked

Supine where torrents pour
Hellward; on crags that high,
Scarred of the thunder, gore
Heaven: the vulture's eye
Swims, and the harpies' cry
Clangs through the ocean's roar.

Notes of æolian light
Calling it hears *her* lips:
Scorched by her burning white
Arms and her armored hips,
Slimy each monster slips
Back to its native night.

Rules she some brighter star?
Inviolable queen
Of what the destinies are?
She with her light unseen
Leading my life; a sheen
Loftier than beauty far.

Oh! in my dreams she lies
With me and fondles me:
Amaranths are her eyes;
And her hair, shadowy
Curlings of scent; and she
Breathes at my heart and sighs.

If with its slaves I bear
All of life's tyranny,—
Worm for the worm,—I care
Naught if my spirit be
Hers in eternity—
Hers who did make it dare.

THE BEAUTIFUL.

OF moires of placid glitter
　　The moon is knitter,
Under low jade-dark branches
The blue night blanches;
Upon yon torrent's arrow
Gleams sink, as narrow
As each blown tress of some soft sorceress
Spell-haunted slumbering in a wilderness.
　　O soul, who dreamest, ponder:—
　　Thy witch, thy love, what wonder
Of charms conceals her from thee powerless!

　　On balmy lakes of glimmer
　　Cool sheets of shimmer
　　Burn glassy, as if inner
　　Sea-castles,—thinner
　　Than peeled pearl-crystal curlings,—

Through eddy whirlings
Sprayed glow of lucid battlement and spire,
The smoldering silver of their smothered fire.
  And hers, thy love's enchanted,
  Where are her towers planted!—
Heart! that thou could'st besiege them with thy lyre!

  By sands of ruffled beaches?
  On terraced reaches
  Of rolling roses, blowing
  Mouths red as glowing
  Cheeks of the folk of Fairy,
  A palace airy?
With pointed casements, thrusts of piercing light,
Piled full of melody and marble-white?
  Where beauty, veiled and hidden,
  Smiles? who my life hath bidden
Come? by her wisdom accoladed knight?

  The blue night's sweetness settles—
  Like hyacinth petals
  Bowed by a weight of teary
  Dew—dayward. Weary

THE BEAUTIFUL.

    One mocking-bird, moon-saddened,
      Sobs on ; and gladdened,
My soul, dissolving, largens to the lie
Named Death by fearful lips. Love, tell me why
      I may not have thee tender?
      Mix with thee? feel thy splendor
Expand me like a bud beneath God's eye?

OVERSEAS.

WHEN fall winds morns with mist, it seems,
   In soul I am a part of it;
Librating on the humid beams,
   A form of frost, I float and flit
     From dreams to dreams. . . .

An old château sleeps 'mid the hills
   Of France; an avenue of sorbs
Conceals it; drifts of daffodils
   Bloom by a scutcheoned gate with barbs
     Like iron bills.

I pass the gate unquestioned, yet
   I feel announced. Broad holm-oaks make
Dark pools of restless violet.
   Between thick bramble banks a lake—
     As in a net

OVERSEAS.

The tangled scales twist—silvers glad.
   Gray, mossy turrets swell above
The feathering foliage. Leafy clad
   Rise ivied walls. A spot for love,
      The garden sad.

Lean, angular windows, awkward seen
   From distant lanes with hawthorn hedged,
Beam broadly on the nectarine
   Espaliered and the peach-tree, wedged
      Twixt drifts of green.

Cool-babbling a fountain falls
   From gryphons' mouths in porphyry;
Clear-eddying swim its carp; white balls
   Of lilies dip it when the bee
      Hugged in them drawls.

Large butterflies, each with a face
   Of Faery on its wings, recline—
Beheaded pansies blown that chase
   Each other—down the shade and shine
      Boughs interlace.

And roses! roses soft as vair,
  Glorying o'er statues and the old
Brass dial; Pompadours that wear
  Their royalty of purple and gold
    With saucy air.

Her scarf, her lute, whose ribbons breathe
  The perfume of her touch; her gloves,
Modeling the daintiness they sheathe;
  Her fan, a Watteau, gay with loves,
    Lie there beneath

A bank of eglantines that heaps
  A sunny blondness. Naïve-eyed,
With lips as suave as they, she sleeps,
  The romance by her open wide
    O'er which she weeps.

PORPHYROGENITA.

I

WAS it when Kriemhild was queen
    Leoëlla?—have forgotten:—
Rode we through the Rhineland seen
    Of a low moon white as cotton?
I, a knight or troubadour?
Thou, a princess tho' a poor
    Damsel of the Royal Closes?
I have dreamed it somewhere sure
    Reading of Kriemhilda's roses.

II

Or from Venice with thee fled
    To the Levant, Graciosa?
Thou, some doge's daughter dead—
    Titian painted thee or Rosa?—

I, that gondolier whose barque
Glided by thy palace dark—
   Near San Marco? Casa d'Oro?—
All thy casement sprang a-spark
   At my barcarolle's *"Te oro."*

III

Klaia, one of Egypt, yea,
   Languid as its sacred lily,
Didst with me a year and day
   Love upon the Isle of Philæ?
I—a priest of Isis? Sweet,
'Neath the date-palms did we meet
   By a temple's pillared marble?
While from its star-still retreat
   Sunk the nightingale's wild warble?

IV

Have I dreamed it?—I, a slave;
   From thy lattice, O Sultana!
Veilless, thy slight hand did wave
   Me a Persian rose, sweet manna
Of thy lips' kiss in its heart?

And through my Chaldæan art,
  With thy Khalif's bags of treasure,
From Damascus did we start
  Westward to some land of pleasure?

V

Was it thou or haply thou?—
  Thou or thou, thou wast so dearest
That thy memory holds me now
  Like a passion; lying nearest
To dead evolutions of
Death to life and life to love:
  Truth invisible but clearest
To the soul that looks above.

ORIENTAL ROMANCE.

BEYOND lost seas of summer she
   Dwelt on an island of the sea,
Last scion of that dynasty,
Queen of a race forgotten long.—
With lips of light and eyes of song,
From seaward groves of blowing lemon,
She called me in her native tongue,
Low-leaned on some rich robe of Yemen.

I was a king. Three moons we drove
Across green gulfs, the crimson clove
And cassia spiced, to meet her love.
Stuffed was my barque with gums and gold,
Strips of rare sandalwood grown old
With odor; and pink pearls of Oman,
Large as her nipples virgin-cold,
   And myrrh less fragrant than this woman.

From Bassora I came. We saw
Her condor castle, on a claw
Of savage precipice, o'erawe
Besieging of the roaring spray;
Like some white opal rough it lay
Above us, all its towers a-taper,
Wherefrom, like an aroma, day
Struck splintered lights of sapphirine vapor.

Lamenting caverns dark, that keep
Sonorous beatings of the deep,
Moaned demon-haunted 'neath the steep.
Fair as the moon whose beams are shed
In Ramadan, the queen, who led
My soul unto her island bowers,
I found—yea, lying young and dead
Among her maidens and her flowers.

LOVE I HAD BANISHED.

LOVE I had banished away for a day,
   Banished a thorn to the thorns of Scorn,
Passing, behold how he lay like a ray,
Lay like the creamiest cluster of may,
   Clad on with myrrh and with morn!

Stricken of bitterness fleet were my feet,
   Fleet to the side which my heart had denied;
Fain for his laughter, a seat at his sweet
Side, and hard kisses to heal him and heat
   The ice of his wounded pride.

Holding him there, with the night lying light
   As plumes that are stirred of a sleeping bird;
Crushing him close to me, slight beat the white
Rose of his members, like rain that is bright
   'Neath the sun riding kingly and spurred.

LOVE I HAD BANISHED.

Kissing him there in the glow and the blow,
    Glow of the blue and blow of the dew,
Leaned to him, happy and slow as the flow
Of stars that thirst trembling through darkness,
    Blush was his cheeks' hale hue. [leaned low,

Blossoming limbs that breathed rare, and as bare
    As beauty who dreams in the gray moonbeams;
Glamorous gold fell his hair that was fair
Lit of his eyes, starring lustrous the lair
    Of curls that were shadowy gleams.

Love, I had taken for mate, as the late
    Hours crept slow through the shy night's glow,
Stole from me leaving a weight as of fate,
Fate and all scorn, and the harshness of hate,
    Hard on my slumbering woe.

Love, I had held to my breast and caressed,
    Hiding him deep in the eyes of sleep,
Waking had flown from the nest he had pressed,
Pressed with his fondling limbs, and the rest—
    Remembrance that only can weep.

HE TELLS.

I

YOU ask how I knew that I knew it?—
    Like the king in an Asian tale,
I wandered on deserts that panted
With noon to a castle enchanted,
    That Afrits had reared in a vale;
    A vale where the sunlight lay pale
As moonlight. And round it and through it
    I searched and I searched. Like the tale

II

No eunuch black-browed as a Marid
    Prevented me. Silences seemed—
Nude slaves with the kohl and the henné
In eyes and on fingers—so many
    White whispers in dimness that dreamed

Where censers of ambergris steamed :
And I came on a colonnade quarried
   From silvery marble, it seemed.

III

And here a wide court rose estraded :
   Fierce tulips, like carbuncles, bloomed
Mid jonquil and jessamine glories;
Strange birds like the cockatoos, lories,
   Spread wings, like great blossoms, illumed,
   Or splashed in the fountain perfumed ;
Kept captive by network of braided
   Spun gold where low galleries gloomed.

IV

From nipples of five bending Peries
   Of gold that was auburn, in rays
The odorous fountain sprang calling :
I heard through the white water's falling—
   More sweet than the laughter of sprays,
   Than songs of our happiest days—
A music sighed soft, as if fairies
   Touched wind-harps whose chords were of rays.

V

I searched through long corridors paneled
   With sandal, whose doorways hung draped
With stuffs of the Chosroës, garded
With Indian gold. Up the corded
   Stone stairway's bronze dragons that gaped;
Through moon-spangled hangings escaped—
Twixt pillars of juniper channeled—
   To a room constellated and draped.

VI

As in legends—of visions a vassal
   One hears, yet beholds naught, and hears
A voice that encourages yearnings;—
More subtle than aloes-wood burnings,
   The chamber sings filled for the ears
With melody; nothing appears:—
My life found your soul such a castle,
   Your love is the music it hears.

SHE SPEAKS.

LAST night you told me where we, parting, waited,
   Of love somehow I'd known before you told—
Long, long ago this love, perhaps, was fated,
   For why was it made suddenly so old?

"Dear things we have and in their own truth cherish,
   Born with us seem, and as ourselves shall last?
Part of our lives we can not let them perish
   Out of our present's future or its past?"

Then is it strange, dazed by that wider wonder,
   I, walking in the woods the morrow's dawn,
Should marvel not that by my feet and under,
   The wildflowers now were purer than those gone?

The woodbird's silver warble sunk completer?
  The sun whirled whiter, lordlier o'er the noon?
That night, sweet God! hung starrier, holier, sweeter,
  In Babylonian witchcraft of the moon?

All love hath emanations: an ideal
  Beats, beats within all beauty. I was moved
No more when, dreamed, my spiritual dream rose real,
  Than by what virtue, God divined, I loved.

UNCERTAINTY.

IT will not be to-day and yet
  I think and dream it will; and let
The slow uncertainty devise
So many sweet excuses met
With many dull confuting lies.

The panes were sweated with the dawn:
Through their drilled dimness, shriveled drawn,
The aigret of one princess-feather,
One monk's-hood tuft with oilets wan,
I glimpsed, dead in the slaying weather.

This morning when my window's chintz
I drew—how gray the day was!—since
I saw him, yea, all days are gray!—
I gazed out on my dripping quince
Defruited, torn, then turned away

UNCERTAINTY.

To weep and did not weep, but felt
A colder anguish than did melt
About the tearful-visaged year.
Then flung the casement wide and smelt
The Autumn sorrow: Rotting near

The rain-soaked sunflowers, wooden bleached,
Up whose poor bodies ashen reached
Nipped morning-glories, seeded o'er
With dangling aiglets, whence beseeched
One blue bloom's brilliant palampore.

The podded hollyhocks, vague, tall,
Wind-battered sentries, by the wall
Rustled their tatters; dripped and dripped
The fog thick on them. Dying all
The tarnished, drooping zinneas tipped.

I felt the death and loved it; yea,
To have it nearer, sought the gray,
Chill, fading close. Yet could not weep;
But only sigh some "well-a-way,"
And yearn with heaviness to sleep.

UNCERTAINTY.

Mine were the fog, the frosty stalks,
The weak lights on the leafy walks,
The shadows shivering with the cold;
The torpid cricket's dreary talks,
The last, dim, ruined marigold.

But when to-night the moon swings low—
A great marsh-marigold of glow—
And all my garden with the sea
Moans, then the palmer mist, I trow,
A shadow'll bring to comfort me.

FALL.

FAR off a wind sprung, and I heard
    Wide oceans of the woods reply—
The herald of some royal word
    From bannered trumpet blown to die
        On hills that held the sky.

The pomp of forests seemed to meet
    Bluff monarchs on a cloth of gold,
Where berries of the bitter-sweet,
    Which, splitting, show the coals they hold,
        Sowed gems of topaz old.

Where, under tents of maples, bredes
    Of smooth carnelians oval, red
The spice-bush spangled; where, like beads,
    The dog-wood's rounded rubies –fed
        With color—blushed and bled.

So with my dream my soul went out,
   And marked, mid richness cavalier,
A minne-singer—lips a-pout;
   A voice of sleep and sunlight clear;
     A rose stuck in his ear:

Eyes dancing, like old German wine,
   All mirth and moonlight; naught to spare
Of slender beard, that curls a line
   Above his lip—bow humbly there
     A hazel heap of hair.

His blue baretta's sweeping plume
   A gleam of whiteness droops; his hose,
Puffed at the thighs, of purple loom;
   His tawny doublet, slashed with rose,
     A dangling dagger shows;

A slim lute slants his breast. I hear
   The leaf-crisp coming of his foot—
No wonder that the regnant Year
   Bends on his beauty blushes mute,
     And sighs to be his lute.

BENEATH THE BEECHES.

I

I LONG, oh long to lie
 'Neath beechen branches, twisted
Green twixt the summer sky;
The woodland shadows nigh—
Brown dryads sunbeam-wristed:—
The live-long day to dream
Beside a wildwood stream.

II

I long, oh long to hear
The claustral forest's breathings,
Sounds soothing to the ear;
The yellow-hammer near,
Beam-bright, thrid wild-vine wreathings:
The live-long day to cross
Slow o'er the nut-strewn moss.

III

I long, oh long to see
The nesting red-bird singing
Glad on the wood-rose tree;
To watch the breezy bee,
Half in the wild-flower, swinging;
God's live-long day to pass
Deep in cool forest grass.

IV

Oh you, so belted in
With mart and booth and steeple,
Brick alley-ways of Sin,
What hope for you to win
Ways free of pelf and people!
Ways of the leaf and root
And soft Mygdonian flute!

ANDALIA.

I

SONG, that did waken you,
  Song, that had taken you,
Has not forsaken you:
  Still with the Spring
My mad and merriest
Part of the veriest
Season and cheeriest;
  You, who can bring
Airs that the birds have taught you;
Grace that the winds have brought you;
Mien that the lilies laughed you;
Thoughts that the high stars waft you—
  Are you a human thing?

II

Dreams—are you aught with them?
You who are fraught with them;
You, like their thought, with them
   Beautiful too.
Life—you're a gleam of it;
Love—you're a dream of it;
Hope—you're a beam of it
   Bound in the blue
Gray of big eyes that are often
Laughter and languor; that soften
On to me sweetly and slowly
Out with your soul that is holy,
   So purer than dew.

III

Face, like the sweetest of
Perfumes, completest of
Flowers God's fleetest of
   Months ever bear.
Sleep, who walk crisper, sleep,
Than the frost, lisper sleep,

Have you a whisper, sleep,
　　Soft as her hair?
Night and the stars did spin it;
Stars and the night are in it;
Let but one ray of it bind me,
And, did the blind Fates blind me,
　　Fair I should know her, fair!

IV

Love—has it mated you?
Love, that has waited you,
Love, that was fated you
　　Here for a while.
Song, can you sing in me
Fuller, or bring in me
Peace, that will cling in me
　　So through all trial,
Such as her smile? like the morning's—
Fashioning luminous warnings,
Rose, of a passion unspoken:
Love, 't is your seal and its token—
　　The light of her smile.

NOËRA.

NOËRA, when sad Fall
    Has grayed the fallow;
Leaf-cramped the wood-brook's brawl
    In pool and shallow;
When sober wood-walks all
    Strange shadows hallow:

Noëra, when gray gold
    And golden gray
The crackling hollows fold
    By every way,
Thee shall these eyes behold,
    Dear bit of May?

When webs are cribs for dew,
    And gossamers,
Long streaks of silver-blue;

When silence stirs
One dead leaf's rusting hue
Among crisp burs.

Noëra, in the wood
 Or mid the grain,
Thee, with the hoiden mood
 Of wind and rain
Fresh in thy sunny blood,
 Sweetheart, again?

Noëra, when the corn
 Reaped on the fields
Deep aster stars adorn
 With purple shields,
Defying the forlorn
 Decay death wields:

Noëra, haply then,
 Thou being with me,
Each ruined greenwood glen
 Will bud and be
Spring's with the Spring again,
 The Spring in thee.

NOËRA.

Thou of the breezy tread,
　Feet of the breeze;
Thou of the sun-beam head,
　Heart like a bee's;
Face like a woodland-bred
　Anemone's.

Thou to October's death
　An April part
Bring, while she taketh breath
　Against Death's dart;
Noëra, one who hath
　Made mine a heart.

Come with our golden year,
　Come as its gold:
With thy same laughing, clear,
　Loved voice of old;
In thy cool hair one dear,
　Wild marigold.

JULIA.

I

YOU, who know such Mays as blow
    The cowslips by the ways, dear,
The mountain-pink whose heart, you'd think,
The thorn-pierced sparrow's blood did drink,
In their wise way, how—can you say?—
    Is it you're like such Mays, dear?
In moods that run from shade to sun,
A thoughtful gloom; like wild perfume,
A winning smile that laughs down guile—
    Dear day! so go such days, dear.

II

In you some song keeps trying long,
    Like some song bird, for flight, child;
And when you speak all up your cheek
A crystal blush will faintly flush

So saintly sweet! and at your feet
    All shadow turns to light, child.
You may not know, but it is so,
If you but look, hark! far a brook
Foams white through buds! for of the woods
    I know you are some sprite, child.

III

Yes, yes; I swear that what's your hair
    Is but the soft-spun wind, love:
Why, when you move it is as Love
Hid in your grace and feet to face
Peeped roguishly; and well I see
    This Love is not a blind Love.
Laugh, and I hear, in each pink ear
Wood-blossoms strain, dew-words of rain
Slip musical, for you are all
    Of music to my mind, love.

LORA.

I

LORA is her name that slips
Nearly love between the lips;
You must know she is so wise
All she does is lift her eyes
At her name and that replies—
    She's so wise, is Lora.

II

Lora is her name that makes
All the heart a chord that shakes;
When she speaks, she is so blessed,
Life's hard riddle none has guessed
Softens, and the soul's caressed
    By the words of Lora.

III

Lora is her name that brings
Kisses as of airy things.
Honied hum of bees that deep
In the rumpled blue-bells creep,
Buoyant sun-hearts forests keep
For their shadows' lives, such leap
    In the life of Lora.

IV

Lora, when I find your face,
Round your white neck I will lace
One firm arm, and so will woo
Your small mouth, as fresh as dew,
With quick kisses, love, that you
Follow must where hearts are true,
    Somewhere, somewhere, Lora.

BLANCH.

BLANCH is adorable and wise
    As—glad winds teaching birds to sing:
Steal thou and gaze deep in her eyes;—
Such scholars of the starry skies!
    —Canst marvel at the thing?

Nay. Blanch, like some red bud that blows,
    Hoards honey in her sunny heart:
Study her smile; wouldst not suppose
She from some warm, white, serious rose
    Had learned the happy art?

Aye. Words that tarry on her tongue
    Fall more than musical thereof:
And why? 'T is this: her soul was strung
A harp at birth to hope that sung,
    Now hope is joined with love.

PHYLLIS.

I

IF I were her lover
I'd wade through the clover
Over five fields or more;
Over the meadows
To stand with the shadows,
The shadows that circle her door.
I'd walk through the clover
    Yes, by her;
And over and over
    I'd sigh her,
"Your eyes are as brown
As a Night's looking down
On waters that sleep
With the moon in their deep . . ."
    If I were her lover to sigh her.

II

If I were her lover
I'd wade through the clover
Over five fields or more;
And deep in the thickets
Or there by the pickets,
White pickets that fence in her door,
I'd lean in the clover—
    The crisper
For the dews that are over—
    And whisper,
"Your lips are as rare
As the dewberries there,
Half ripe and as red,
On the honey-dew fed—"
    If I were her lover to whisper.

III

If I were her lover
I'd wade through the clover
Over five fields or more;
And watch in the twinkle

Of stars that sprinkle
The paradise over her door.
And there in the clover
    I'd reach her;
And over and over
    I'd teach her,
A love without sighs,
Of laughterful eyes,
That reckoned each second
The pause of a kiss,
A kiss and . . . that is
    If I were her lover to teach her.

VALKYRIEN.

I

NEVER a thought of aught save slaughter,
   Slaughter that smears the spears that thunder!
Anger of ax that shines, like a water
   Gashed in the night of the levin's wonder.
Darts in the eye and their bleak barbs bristling,
   Shaking the heart ere the lance hath stroken;
Hum of arrows and broad-swords' whistling;
   Strength, like an ash, unbowed, unbroken.
By the eye of Odin, whose frown is war!—
Think of the vikings' daughters who wear
Gold on their hips, and the weights of their hair
Gold-bound red as the beard of Thor!
The virgin who brims in the well her jar—
To rape then butcher! a kingdom's ravish
Yours for the sweat and the blood you lavish!

II

Wraths are the pinions of Hate who clamors—
  Hooked wings hovering over the carrion,—
Joy of the blade the helm that hammers!—
  Songs of slaughter: The gnarling clarion
Rings to the revel and sings: with strangling
  Fury it fires the brain to battle:
Strength shocks strength: in its brass bray wrangling
  Smiters are smitten: the harsh hills rattle,
The hard seas rumble, the sharp winds wail.
Think!—were it better by hollow-eyed Hel
To rot with cowards? or boast and yell
Hoarse toasts o'er skulls of the boisterous ale
High in Valhalla, where life wends well!—
The warrior vault of its shields wild curses
Laughs to the roar of the berserk verses !

MOTHS.

I

O, when the fiery
Glow-worm in briery
Banks of the moon-mellowed bowers
Sparkles—so hazily
Pinioned and airily
Delicate!—warily
Float to buds, lazily,
Moths that are kin to the flowers.

II

White as the dreamiest
Beams that the creamiest
Rose of the garden that dozes
Nestles; that burn in it,
Held in the heart of its
Heart like a part of its
Perfume, to turn in it
Dew, flit the moths to the roses.

III

Slow as the forming of
Dew in the warming of
Stars, brush their mouths on the petals;
  Open these swing to them,
    Deep to their sunniest
    Soul, where the honeiest
  Spice is, to fling to them
Nard through the twilight that settles. . . .

IV

So to all tremulous
Souls come the emulous
Angels of Love. Else would perish,
  Crushed, all the good in such:
    Touched, the pure presence of
    Love to the essence of
  Light, a white flood, in such
Flatters—aroma they cherish.

AS IT IS.

MAN'S are the learnings of his books—
    What is all knowledge that he knows
Beside the wit of winding brooks,
    The wisdom of the summer rose!

How soil distils the scent in flowers
    Baffles his science: Heaven-dyed,
How, from the palette of His hours,
    God colors gives them, hath defied.

What broad religion of the light,
    Ere stars in heaven beat burning tunes,
Stains all the hollow edge of night
    With glory as of molten moons?

Why sorrow is more strange than mirth,
    And death than birth? and afterward,
What sweetness in the bitter earth
    Makes life's mortality so hard?

THOUGHTS.

I

How the may-apple or
    Solitude cyclamen—
Star-perfect as a star—
    In woodland glade and glen,
Blossoms when breezes woo,
With language of the dew,
Up to the broken blue
Of lonesome skies, do you
    Know or do I, love?

II

Can wild anemones
    Think?—for they tremble so;
As if two cousin bees
    This side then that bent low.—

When the soft sunlight links,
Braided of dew-drop winks,
Crowns 'round each head that shrinks,—
What its heart's aura thinks
   Know you or I, love? . . .

III

Know, when the Springtide trod
   By in a blowing blush,
Wise as a gaze of God
   Holding all Heaven a-hush,
Love was her thought and love
Through the vast soul above
Wrought so, they sprang thereof,
Thought into thoughts, were wove
   Symbols of living love.

AFTER THE TOURNAMENT.

I

AND shall it be when white thorns flake
  With blossoms all the budding brake,
The rustle of one lifting leaf
  Will whisper low;
And one be near thee as thy grief—
  And wilt thou know?

II

Or shall it be, when blows and dies
The forest columbine, two eyes
  Will bloom against thine faint as frost?
    Thou, deep in dreams,
  Wilt hark what plaintive winds sigh, lost
    In life that seems?

III

Or shall it be where rocks slope, smooth
With water-wear, where vague lights soothe;
  One in an old lute will beseech
    Thy listening ears
  With Provence melodies, that reach
    The soul like tears?

IV

Yes; this will be—Loop thy white arm
Beneath my hair . . . so; let thy warm
  Blue eyes dream on me for a space,
    A little while;
  Love, it will rest me; and thy face—
    Ah, let it smile.

V

Now art thou thou. Yet—let thy hair
A golden fragrance fall; thy fair
  Full throat bend low; thy kiss be hot
    With life not dry
  With anguish. Sweet my Evalott!
    Now let me die.

AMONG THE ACRES OF THE WOOD.

I

I KNOW, I know,
   The way doth go,
Athwart a greenwood glade, oh!—
White gleam the wild-plumes in that glade,
White as the bosom of the maid
Who stooping sits and milks and sings
Among the dew-dashed clover-rings,
When fades the flush, the henna-blush,
   Of evening's glow, an orange slow,
And all the winds are are laid, oh!

II

I wot, I wot,
   And is it not
Right o'er the viney hill?
Say! where the wild-grapes mat and make
Penthouses to each bramble-brake,

And dangle plumes of fragrant blooms?
Where leaking sunbeams string the glooms
With beryl beads? where sprinkled weeds
   Blue blossoms fill? and shrill, oh shrill,
   Sings all night long one whippoorwill?

III

   I ween, I ween
   The path is green
'Neath beechen boughs that let
Gay glances of the bashful sky
Gleam usward like a girlish eye.
At night one far and lambent star
Shines limpid, like a watching Lar;
'Mid branching buds a tangled bud.
Where in the acres of the wood
   Blow strips of wet, wild violet,
   There only we have trysting met.

LOVE A-MILKING.

I

"HOARD no more hope! believe me!"
—"Thou wouldst not make me poor!"—
"Wouldst lead me to deceive me?
　As many a maid before,
To win me then to leave me?—
　Say no more, sir, say no more!"

"Love trusts! sweet faith! thereof, my lass,
　Trust wins to trust above, my lass—
Love's older than our love, my lass,
　Not wiser than of yore."

II

"Thy love is over simple
　To woo one on the leas;
One's kirtle torn; in wimple
　Unbusked; tanned by the breeze."
—"Thou needest but that dimple—
　On thy knees, Love, on thy knees!

"What's wiser than thine eyes, my lass?
Thy heart?—Beneath God's skies, my lass,
Love! wiser than the wise, my lass—
We blind! 'tis Love who sees.

III

"'Low apple blossoms breaking
Pay me the kiss dost owe."
—"'Tis thine, thine be the taking."
—"Aboon the afterglow
Three kiss-soft stars are waking—
Walk slow, my love, walk slow."

"More dear the dusk for dew, my lad;
More sweet the stars when few, my lad;
Life's trials, when love is true, my lad,
Are lighter than we know."

ROMANTIC LOVE.

I

IS it not sweet to know?—
 The moon hath told me so—
That in some lost romance, love,
Long lost to us below,
A knight with casque and lance, love,
A thousand years ago,
I kissed you from a trance, love,—
 The moon hath told me so.

II

Or were it strange to wis?
The stars have told me this—
Once sang a nightingale, love,
On some old isle of Greece;
A wizard loved its wail, love,

That it might never cease,
From the full notes a woman,
More lovely than one human,
Devised—so goes the tale, love,—
　The stars have told me this.

III

Is it not quaint to tell?—
The flowers remember well—
Was once a rose that blew, love,
Pale in a haunted dell;
And one, a Fairy true, love,
By loving broke the spell,
And lo! the rose was—you, love,—
　The flowers remember well.

IV

To moon and flower and star
We are not what we are:
Sometimes, from o'er that sea, love,
Whose scolloped sands are far—
From shores of Destiny, love,—

ROMANTIC LOVE.

The winds that wing and war,
Will waft a thought that glistens
To memory who listens,
Reminding thee and me, love,
  We are not what we are.

PASTORAL LOVE.

THE pied pinks tilt in the wind that worries—
   Oh, the wind and the tan o' her cheek;
And the close sun sleeps on the rye nor hurries—
   And what shall a lover speak?

The toad-flax flowers in flaxen hollows—
   Oh, the bloom and her yellow hair;
And the greenwood brook a wood-way follows—
   'Shall say to the shy and fair?

The gray trees stoop where the daylight sprinkles—
   Hey, the day and the shine i' her eye;
And a gray bird pipes and a wild brook tinkles—
   And what may a maid reply?

Hey, the hills when the evening settles!
  Oh the Edens within her eyes!
Say, the tryst mid the dropping petals!
  Lo, the low replies!

"Yes, when the west is a blur of roses"—
  But what o' the buds o' thy cheeks, my dear?
"Yes, when there's rest and the twilight closes"—
  "And love is breathed in the ear."

IMMORTAL.

"ASK what thou wilt! long hast thou lived with flowers
      And dreams and trod the way
      Of pleasure—for one ray?—
Ask what thou wilt of all thy lived-out hours."

And shall it be, when stooping to me there
      He said, "She sleeps," and I
      Dreaming divined his sigh,
And felt fierce lips moist-crushed to mouth and hair?

No: Shall it be, when that mad night his fingers
      Held from my brow the curls,
      Dropping like unstrung pearls
Words of his love fell—words whose memory lingers?

No: Shall it be, when, while the distant sea
    Gleamed, folded breast to breast,
    With hope his heart expressed,
"Such all thy present, O futurity!"

No: Shall it be, when, belted with his arms,
    Looked in my soul his soul,
    Embracing with the whole
Truths of our eyes, our lives laughed drugged with charms?
No! No!—that hour wherein he left me lost!
    Stunned, fallen and despised
    Before the world he prized,
When, God forgive me! when I loved him most!

SLEEP.

LOOK in my eyes! oh the mild and mysterious
    Deeps of thy eyes that are holy with rest!—
Sigh to me! yes, as thy cousin, imperious
Love, might, with lips that are soft and delirious,
    Soft with such pureness as blesses the blessed.
Fold all my soul in the mild and mysterious
        Might of thy rest.

All the night for thy love, all the night! while the
    gladdening
    Presence of dark as a legend of old
Speaks in me poesy; none of the saddening
Prose of the day that is sad with the maddening
    Heart of unrest that is heartless and cold.
All the night for thy love, all the night! and its
    gladdening
        Beauty of old.

SLEEP.

Scorn is not thine, nor is hate; but the bubbling
    Fountains of strength that are youthful with morns;
Hurt is not thine of remembrance; the troubling
Bruises of waking whose fingers keep doubling—
    Doubling on temples life's cares that are thorns.
Thine are the hours of the stars and the bubbling
    Wells of the morns.

Pride and the passion of greed that do worry us,
    Mix with and brutalize; sorrow and spite
At the heart that's an-ache with the tears that will
    hurry us
On in the iron of anguish to bury us—
    Touch them and calm with thy fingers of white.
Make all these passions and pains, that do worry us,
    Night with the night.

Thine are the mansions of slumber; the flowery
    Fields of the visions that blossom the dreams;
Thine the high mountains of peace that lie showery
Under the stars; and the valleys of bowery,
    Balmy forgettings made misty with streams.
Thine the white halcyon mansions, the flowery
    Pastures of dreams.

Stay for me; stand by me; stoop to me; pray for me!
 Pray, my Madonna, the incense of prayer!
Mother of hope! whose kind eyes are a-ray for me,
Vestal with goodness, that fills all the day for me
 New with a vigor that masters despair.
Stay for me; be of me breath of me; pray for me,
 Sister of Prayer!

GHOSTLY WEATHER.

SPITE'S flaws of drizzle hoot and hiss
Through dodging lindens whistled through:
The dead's own days be days like this—
Yea: let me sit and be with you,

Here in your willow-chair whose seat
Spreads scarlet plush. Hark! how the gusts
In sad æolian cracks repeat
Mild moans. They haunt your rooms, whose dusts

Wan-wind each ornament and chair:
That locked in memory where you died.
Since angels stood there saintly fear
Guards each dark angle, mournful-eyed.

Through this dim eve stoop your dim face;
Gray gaze, like rain-drops', dimly deep;
A soft gray cloudiness of lace,
Stand near me while I sleep, I sleep.

THE BRIDLE-PATH.

I

THROUGH meadows of the iron-weeds,
   Whose purple blooms flash, slipping
Twice-twinkling drops of dewy beads,
The thin path twists and winding leads
   Through woodland hollows dripping;
Down to a creek with bedded reeds;
On to the lilied dam that feeds
The mill, whose wheel through willow-bredes
   Winks, the white water whipping.

II

It wends through meads of mint and brush
   Where silvery seeds sink drowsy,
Or sail along the heatful hush:
Past where the bobwhite in the bush
   Has built a nest, and frowsy

Hides calling clear. A split through crush
Of crowded saplings low and lush;
A seam by pools of flag and rush
   Where blows the brier-rose blowsy.

III

Across the ragweed fallow-lot
   Whose low rail-fence encumbers
The dense-packed berries ripening hot;
Where on the summer one far spot
   Of gray the gray hawk slumbers.
Then in the greenwood where the rot
Of leaves and loam smells cool; and shot
With dotting dark the touch-me-not
   Swings curling horns in numbers.

IV

Around brown rocks that bulge and lie
   Deep in damp ferns and mosses,—
Like giants, each lounged on his thigh
To watch some forest quarry die,—
   The path toils steep; then crosses

A bramble-bridge; up-whirring nigh
A wood-dove startles, 'thwart the sky
A jarring light: rock-babbling by
    The brook its diamonds tosses.

V

Ho! through the wildwood then we go
    In pulse of shade and singing;
Where pale-pink sorrel-grasses grow;
The vari-colored toadstools sow
    And swell dark soils, bestringing
Rough red-oak roots. Where, swinging low
Their green burs, limbs rub when each slow
Faint forest wind sounds. Fresh the flow
    Of hidden waters ringing.

VI

While far away among the cane,
    Or spice-bush belts, the tinkle
Of one stray bell drifts yet again,
Lost near some lone and leafy lane
    Where smooth the red ruts wrinkle. . . .

Fills all the skies a grayish stain
   Of smoky blue. A hint of rain.
The sun is hid. Hard down the grain
   A gust dents; and a sprinkle

VII

The dimpled dust has drilled. Hark!—one
   Big mouthful of the thunder—
Gruff. Scurrying with the dust we run
Into a whiff of hay and sun,
   Of cribs and barns; and under
The martin-builded eaves, where dun
The sparrows house with fussy fun,
"Will it be done soon as begun?"
   We wonder and we wonder.

VIII

A crashing wedge of stormy light
   Vibrating blinds, and dashes
A monster elm to splinters white.
Hush: then a fit of rain that bright
   The tumbled straw-stacks lashes.

The rain is over. Left and right
Foregathering gales of green delight,
Fresh rain-scents of each holt and height
   Where each blade drips and flashes.

IX

A ghostly gold grows slowly through
   The crumbled clouds; and woven
From rainy rose to rainy blue
A strange, sweet dotting as of dew
   Dies into trembling doven.
High-buoyed in rack now one or two
White stars shine slight—the pirate clew
To Night's rich hoard. The west's a hue
   Of bruised pomegranate cloven.

NOONING.

I

WEAK winds that make the water wink,
    White clouds that sail from lands of Fable
To white Utopias vague, and sink
Down gulfs of blue unfathomable:
        Their rolling shadows drifting
        O'er fields of forest lifting
Wild peaks of purple range that loom and link.

II

Warm knolls whereon the Nooning dreams;
In droning dells that bask in brightness,
Low-lulled with hymns of mountain streams'
Far-foaming falls of windy whiteness;
        Where from the glooming hollow,
        With cawing crows that follow,
The hunted hawk wings wearily and screams.

III

Thick-buzzing heat the dryness fills
Where ever some hoarse locust's whirring;
No answering voice shouts in the hills
Receding echoes far-recurring—
  As when the dawning dimpled,
  With hazel twilight wimpled,
From dewy tops called o'er responding rills.

IV

Wan with sweet summer tips the deep
Hot heaven with the high sun hearted—
A wide May-apple bloom asleep
With golden-pistiled petals parted.—
  Now, could befall,—her pouting
  Cheeks anger-red—from sprouting
Rock-mosses some white wildwood dream might leap.

THE LOG-BRIDGE.

I

LAST month, where the low log-bridge is laid
    O'er the woodland brook, in the belts o' the shade,
To the right, to the left pink-packed, was made
    A gloaming glory of scented tangle
By the bramble-roses deep—that wade
High-heaped on the sides—when they bloomed to fade,
And wilting powdered the ruts, and swayed
    To the waters beneath loose loops of spangle:
Wide eyes of buff which the pale lids braid,
    Murmurous-soft with the bees a-wrangle.

II

This month—'t is August—the lane that leads
To the bramble-bridge runs waste with weeds,
That lift bright saffron. Light satin seeds
    Of thistle-fleece blow by you hazy;

Starry the hedge with the thousand bredes
Of the yellow daisy—like sweet-eyed creeds
Peacefully praying;—now by you speeds
    A butterfly sumptuous with mottle and lazy.
Dull yellowish-white, where the blue-bird pleads,
    The sumach's tassel tilts low as the daisy.

III

All golden the spot in the noon's gold shine,
Where the yellow-bird sits with eyes of wine
And swings and whistles; where line on line
    In coils of warmth the sunbeams nestle;
Where cool by the pool (where the crawfish, fine
As a shadow's shadow, darts dim) to mine
The damp creek-clay, with their peevish whine
    Come mason-hornets and roll and wrestle
Wet balls of earth to their breasts, and twine
    Cylindrical nests on the joists o' the trestle.

IV

Where the horsemint shoots through the grasses high,
On the root-thick rivage that roofs, a dry
Gray knob that bristles with pink, the sigh
    Of crickets is sharp 'neath the dead leaves' bosoms.

THE LOG-BRIDGE.

At twilight sad you will hear the cry
Of a passing bird flit twittering by;
And the frogs' grave antiphons rise and die;
    And here to drink come the wild opossums,
Where lithe on those roots two lizards lie
    Brown-backed like the bark, or stir the blossoms.

THE OLD FARM.

DORMERED and verandaed cool,
   Locust-girdled on the hill,
Stained with weather-wear and full
   Of weird whispers, at the will
Of the sad winds' rise and lull;

I remember, stood it there
   Brown above the woodland deep
In a scent of lavender,
   With slow shadows locked in sleep,
Or the warm light everywhere.

I remember how the spring,
   Liberal-lapped, bewildered its
Squares of orchard murmuring;
   Kissed with budded puffs and bits,
Where the wood-thrush came to sing.

THE OLD FARM.

Barefoot so at first she trod,
  A pale beggar maid, adown
The quaint quiet, till the god
  With the seen sun for a crown
And the firmament for rod,

Graced her nobly, wedding her—
  Her Cophetua; and so
All the hill, one breathing blur,
  Burst in blossom; peachy blow;
Wonderstricken whiteness pure.

Seckel, blackheart, palpitant
  Rained their bleaching strays; and white
Bulged the damson bent a-slant;
  Russet-tree and romanite
Seemed beneath deep drifts to pant.

And it stood there, brown and gray,
  In the bee-boom and the bloom,
In the murmur and the day,
  In the passion and perfume,
Grave as age among the gay.

Good with laughter romped the clear
    Boyish voices 'round its walls;
Rare wild-roses were the dear
    Girlish faces in its halls,
Music-haunted year to year.

Far before it meadows full
    Of green pennyroyal sank;
Clover dots like bits of wool
    Pinched from lambs; and now a bank
Bright of color; and the cool

Brown-blue shadows undefined
    Of the clouds rolled overhead—
Curdled mists that kept the wind
    Fresh with rain and fluting shed
Song among the valleys kind.

Where in mint and gipsy-lily
    Ran the rocky brook away;
Musical among the hilly
    Solitudes its flashing spray,
Sunlight-soft or forest-stilly.

Buried in thick sassafras,
  Half-way up the copsy hill,
Moved some cowbell's muffled brass;
  And the ruined water-mill
Loomed half-hid in cane and grass.

I remember; stands it yet
  On the hilltop, in the musk
Of damp meads, while violet
  Deepens all the dreaming dusk
Droning over? holy wet.

With the slightest dew? while low
  One long tear of scarlet gashes,
Tattered, the broad primrose glow
  Westward, and in weakest splashes
Lilac stars the heavens sow?

Sleeps it still among its roses
  Dewy yellow, while the choir
Of the lonesome insects dozes?
  And the white moon drifting higher
Brightens and the darkness closes—
Sleeps it still among its roses?

AMONG THE KNOBS.

THERE is a place embanked with brush
    Three wooded knobs beyond,
Lost in a valley where the lush
    Wild eglantine blows blonde.

Where light the dogwoods earliest
    Their torches of white fires,
And bee-bewildered east and west
    The red-haws build their spires.

The wan wild-apples' flowery sprays
    Blur through the misty gloom
A pensive pink; and by lone ways
    The close blackberries bloom.

AMONG THE KNOBS.

I love the spot: A shallow brook
    Slips from the forest near,
Bird-haunted; flags in many a nook;
    Its rustling depths so clear

The minnows glimmer where they glide
    Above its rocky bed—
A long, dear, boyhood's brook, not wide,
    Which has its sparkling head

Among the rainy hills, and drops
    By four low waterfalls—
Wild music of an hundred stops—
    Between the leafy walls

Against the water-gate, that hangs
    A rude portcullis dull
Of wan-washed wood, whose clumsy fangs
    The cress makes beautiful.

The bright green dragon-flies about
    The seeding grasses swim;
The streaked wasps worrying in and out,
    Dart fretfully and slim.

Here in the moon-gold moss that glows
    Like jets of moonlight, dies
The weak anemone; and blows
    Some flower less blue than skies.

And, where in April tenderly
    The dewy primrose made
A thin, peculiar fragrance, we
    In the pellucid shade

Found wild strawberries half-abud;
    In May, long berries fresh
Hung pallid-pink as wood-bird's blood
    On many a trailing mesh.

Once from that hill a farmhouse mid
    Large orchards—cozy brown
In lilacs and brave roses hid—
    With picket-fence looked down.

O'er ruins now the roses guard;
    The plum and seckel-pear
And apricot rot on the sward
    Their wasted ripeness there.

But when low huckleberries blow
   Their waxen bells I 'll tread
Those dear accustomed ways that go
   Dim down that orchard ; led

To that avoided spot which seems
   The haunt of vanished Springs;
Lost as the hills in drowsy dreams
   Of visionary things.

GARGAPHIE.

Succinctæ sacra Dianæ.—OVID.

I

THERE the ragged sunlight lay
   Tawny on thick ferns and gray
      On dark waters; dimmer,
Lone and deep, the cypress grove
Shadowed whisperings and wove
Braided lights, like those that love
On the pearl plumes of a dove
      Pale to gleam and glimmer.

II

There centennial pine and oak
Into stormy basses broke;
      Hollow rocks gloomed slanting
Echoy; in dim arcade
Looming with loose moss that made
Sunshine streaks in tatters laid.
Oft a wild hart, hunt afrayed,
      Plunged the water panting.

III

Poppies of a sleepy gold
Mooned the gold-green twilights old
    Of its vistas, making
Fuzzy puffs of flame. And pale
Stole some slim deer down a dale
Haunting; and the nightingale
Throbbed not near—the olden tale
    All its hurt heart breaking.

IV

There the hazy serpolet,
Glinting cistus, blooming wet,
    Blushed on bank and boulder;
There the cyclamen, as wan
As weak footprints of the Dawn,
Carpeted the spotted lawn;
There the nude nymph, dripping drawn,
    Basked a peachy shoulder.

V

In the citrine shadows there
What tall presences and fair,
    White and godly gracious,
Hidden where the rock-rose grew,

Watched through eyeballs of the dew
Or from sounding oaks, and knew
All the mystery of blue
    Heaven vaulted spacious!

VI

Guarded that Bœotian
Valley so no foot of man
    Soiled its silence holy
With profaning tread—save one,
The Hyantian: Actæon,
He beheld—What god might shun
Fate, Diana's wrath called on,
    With what magic moly!

VII

Lost it lies, like one who sleeps
In serene enchantment. Keeps
    Beautiful in beamy
Beauty of its blooms that be
Wisdoms; hope, its high stars see,
Near in fountains; deity
In wise wind-words of each tree—
    Gargaphie the dreamy.

ROSICRUCIAN.

I

WHEN leas of white-blown clover
   Smell thinly of the rain;
When long drops wrinkle over
   Low lime-leaves in the lane;
Among the dwindling acres
Whence troop the harvest-makers,
Tanned reapers, freckled rakers,
   Wild heart, be wild again.

Where running trumpet-flowers,
   Elf war-horns red as brass,
The old elm swaying showers
   Among its root-grown grass;
Where green the daylight streaming
Sets all the wild-birds dreaming,
Between the real and seeming,
   Dim love, what words shall pass?

ROSICRUCIAN.

When from the mustard fragrant
   Brown bees break rough with gold;
And breezes trailing vagrant
   Spill half the spice they hold;
When heights begin to glimmer,
And shadows, slipping slimmer,
Crouch by the woodland dimmer,
   What secrets shall be told?

II

Where moonbeam-tangled reaches
   A mock-bird fills with moan,
And one fall's breaking bleaches
   A gray glow down its stone;
My soul shall wait to meet you;
My heart shall hold and heat you;
My love shall so complete you
   That death will not be known.

Though of frail mist your members
   That waver faltering white;
Your eyes dark stars whose embers
   Grow gradually bright,

Not mine, dim love, to miss you;
But mine to clasp and kiss you;
Mine well to know this is you,
   To have you with the night.

Lone sings the lonesome cricket;
   Wet, wood aromas smell;
Deep in the shapeless thicket
   The owl the hours doth tell;
Strange love, my lips shall name you—
Though demons rise to shame you
In angels' eyes and blame you—
Of heaven, my heaven, though came you
   From Heaven or from Hell.

HIS SONG.

SING to me how I pine to blow
The flower beneath thy lattice low—
Then wouldst thou cull me, sweet, and wear
A captive in thy slumberous hair,
      Thy hair?

Sing to me how I yearn to shine
Yon pearly star above yon pine
Thou gazest on—I, of the skies,
Should thus be taken to thine eyes,
      Thine eyes?

Sing to me how I'd be the breeze
Which dips the dandelioned leas
Thy footsteps find—I, of the south,
Might live a kiss upon thy mouth,
      Thy mouth?

HIS SONG.

Sing to me how my heart doth long
To be the burden of some song
Thou lovest; so myself might be
The melody of memory
      To thee.

APOCALYPSE.

BEFORE I found you I had found
   Of your true eyes the open book
(Where re-created heaven wound
Its wisdom with it) in the brook.

Ah, when I found you, looking in
Those Scriptures of your eyes, above
All earth, o'ersoared earth's vulture, Sin,
So apotheosized to love.

And searching yet beneath it, saw
The soul impatient of the sod—
What wonder then your love should draw
Me to the nearer love of God.

ILLUSION.

I HAVE loved beauty but to find it mortal—
All dearest things are born but for a tear;
I have loved life whose cold hand points a portal,
    That near, is never near.

I have loved men and learned we are not brothers—
O brother blindness that must end in pain!
I have loved women, more than all the others,
    And found them false and vain.

Made unseen stars my keblahs of devotion;
Prayed for attainment and remained a clod:
Strange gods have worshiped wildly while the ocean
    Told of no god but God.

Then in myself, all world beliefs laid level,
I searched, and found a little jealous dust
Hiding a tiny jewel—Ah! the evil!
    That soiled the soul with lust.

DUTY AND LOVE.

I

WHAT makes thee beautiful,
　　Answer, ah, answer?—
"It is that dutiful
　Souls are all beautiful:
　　'Tis that romance or
　Glamour of spirit
　Hearts of high merit
　Of Heaven inherit—
　　Hast thou an answer?"

II

What makes thee loveable,
　　Answer, ah, answer?—
"Love; for, thereof, able
　Souls are made loveable:
　　'Tis that which chance or
　Birth, of the woman
　Gives to illumine
　That which is human—
　　Hast thou an answer?"

Shapes and Shadows.

BLODEUWEDD.

NOT to that demon's son, whom Arthur erst
    For prophecy, at old Caerleon durst
Grace wisely, Merlin,—not to him alone
Did those lost learnings of high magic, done
With mystery of marvels, then belong:
Taliesin, now, hath told us in a song
Of one at Arvon, Math of Gwynedd, lord
Of some vague cantrevs of the North, whose sword
Beat back and slew the monarch of the South
Through puissance of Gwydion.

                      His mouth
Was wise with wondrous witchcraft; for his word
Wrought the invisible visible and stirred
Eyes with a seeming sight that, so deceived,
The mind conceited shapes and shapes believed;

Wrought flesh creations from air elements,
For, let him wish, the winds were wan with tents,
And brassy blasts of war from bugles brayed,
And shocking hosts of battle clanged and swayed,
And at a word were naught. With little care
Steeds rich-accoutered and pied hounds, as fair,
Limber and wiry as the dogs of Earth,
From forest fungus fashioned and gave birth
To lives of twice twelve hours, wherein they moved
Existences, and form perfections proved. . . .

Now to Caer Dathyl Math through Gwydion,—
The son of Don,—the daughter dark of Don,
The silver-circled Arianrod, had brought;—
A southern rose of beauty, friendship sought
For full espousal. When the maiden came
Said Math, "Art thou a virgin?" like a flame,
Mantling, her answer angered, "Verily,
I know not other, lord, than that I be!"
So wrought he then through magic that the form
Of her boy baby chubby on her arm
Cuddled and cooed. "A Mary? yea!" laughed Math,
"Forsooth, another Mary!" then in wrath

BLODEUWEDD.

Set harsh hands on the babe and fiercely flung
Far in the salt sea; but the hard winds clung
Fast to the Elfin and the lithe waves swept
Him safely strandward dry. Some fishers kept
Him thus unseaed and christened Dylan, Fair
Son of the Wave, and fostered him with care.

Nor really was this hers. But Gwydion,
Brother to Arianrod, before the sun
Had time to touch it with one golden glaive,
Some dim small body on the castle pave
In raven velvet seized; and hiding he
Stole this from court to subtly raise and be
A comely youth. In time to Arianrod
Brought, swearing by the rood and blood of God
This was his sister's son. Quoth she, "More shame
Dost thou disgrace thee with to mix our name
With this dishonor, brother, than myself!"
And waxing wroth burst Gwydion, "The elf
Is thine, God's curse!" and daggered her with looks.
And she in turn waxed fiery saying, "Books
Of wisdom I have read as well as thou!
And, yea, upon thy folly, listen, now

I lay a threefold destiny: The first—
Until I name him, nameless is he!—Cursed
Be they who give him arms with palsy! nor
Shall he bear such until I arm for war:
And lastly, know, however high his birth,
He shall not wed a woman of the Earth,
Malignity! to shame me with thy sin!"
So passed into her tower and locked her in.

But Gwydion, departing with the youth,
Sware he would compass her; if not through truth,
Through wiles of learned magic. And he wrought
So that unbending Arianrod was brought
To name the lad. Again he fashioned that,
Through boisterous enchantments fierce, he gat
Her to give arms. But then, not for his life,
Howbeit, might he get him to a wife.
Persisting desperate, anon the thing
Wrought in him blusterous as an early Spring.

Now Llew the youth was named. And Gwydion
Made his complaint to Math, the mighty son
Of Mathonwy.

BLODEUWEDD.

Said he: "Despair not. We
By charms, illusions and white sorcery
Will seek to make—for have we not such powers?
—A woman for him out of forest flowers."

And so they toiled together one wan night,
When the gray moon hung low and watched, a white,
Wild witch's face behind a mist. They took
Blossoms of briers by a bloomy brook
Shed from the womby hills; and phantom blooms
Of yellow broom that filtered faint perfumes;
Thin, rare, frail primroses of rainy smell,
Weak pink, cirque-clustered in a glow-worm dell;
Wild-apple sprigs that tipsied bells of blaze
And in far, haunted hollows made a haze
Of ghostly, scattered fragrance; plaintive blue
Of hollow harebells hoary with the dew;
Kingcups as golden as the large, low stars;
And lilies which, rolled limpid in long bars
Like sleepy starshine, swayed aslant and spilled
Slim nectar-cups of musk the rain had chilled;
Sweet, wildwood wind-flowers, paly, slight of gloss,
Dimpling rough oak-roots bulging the green moss;

BLODEUWEDD.

Lone on the elfin uplands pulled the buds,
That burned like spurts of moonlight when it suds
The rainy clouds, of blossoming meadow-sweet,
And made a woman tall; from crown to feet
Complete in beauty. One far lovelier
Than Branwen daughter of the gray King Llyr;
Than that dark daughter of Leodegrance,
The stately Gwenhevar. And old romance
Dreamed in the open Bibles of her eyes;
Music her motion; and her speech, soft sighs
Of an acknowledged love for love again;
Yet in her face no least suggested pain,
But hope, high heart, and happiness of life.

So Blodeuwedd they named her and as wife—
Fair aspect of wild flowers baptized with dew—
Gave that next morning to the happy Llew.

THE LADY OF VERNE.

I

LADY VALORA'S villa at Verne,
With its old, low terraces staired with stone;
A statue here and a fluted urn
Under fragrant limes; and the land so lone
With the calling of rooks when the west was a-burn.

My Lady of Verne was tall and fair—
With locks dark hazel, and face white rose;
Why, her long gray eyes and her noble hair,
Her slender lips and her classic nose,
Made song of my heart like a beautiful air.

Down the orchard aisles to a dingled stream
One spring we strolled; and the treey hills
In the south loomed blue as a fairy dream;
And I found for her hair dim daffodils—
Thin cups of gold full of moonish beam.

For her bosom a spray from a hawthorn tree
I tore with words as dead as this tongue;
And the bees in the bloom boomed honeyly
While she laughed at my words and merrily sung,
"*My Lady of Verne, what loves hath she!*"

What to her was the gaze I gave
Of desperate hope in a soul distressed!
Love at her feet cringed dumb as a slave!
Her lips by a laugh more golden were pressed—
Yet her smile waned away like the light from a wave.

And we walked in the sunset. So to her home
We came by the east. Slow settling, drear
With its five faint stars and a crescent of foam,
The twilight dusked. And we heard by the mere
One distant bittern boom and drum.

Can a heart be serious so and gay?—
What a riddle unread was she to me!
When I kissed her fingers and turned away,
"Valora of Verne"—why, what cared she
Though a soft light made her eyes more gray!

Though she lingered to watch me, that might be!—
A slim moonbeam in the woodbine-maze,
When I turned, was her muslin drapery,
Strange white that vanished in haunting haze—
My Lady of Verne, why, what cared she!

II

The sheaves of the Autumn had long lain bound;
The harvests of Autumn had long been past;
And the latest snows fell, deepening around,
And the eery heavens scowled overcast;
And alone in her room Valora I found.

Sad and lovely. The young Earl's bride,—
A queen of dreams,—at an oriel leant,
Pale as the buds on her warm hair tied;
The dented satin, flung stormily, bent
Like beaten silver rippling wide.

I mark, as I steal to her side, two tears
Are vaguely large in her beautiful eyes,
As large and pure as the pearls she wears
On her lace-looped bosom's sanctities:
So I say what I know, "Then, it appears" . . .

And stop with, it seems, my soul in my eyes,—
"That you are not happy, Valora of Verne.
Is there that at your heart which—well, denies
These mocking mummeries? True and stern
Is the voice of the soul that never lies.

"Words of the lips are not words of the heart!
For hearts have a speech so different from speech,
So secret, Valora, too holy for art!—
Never mistaken!—and men could not preach
Mine from that love yours said me a part.

"All! all!—my God!—and my all!—now life
Is what to me and—to you?" She turned
With a hard look saying, "Coward! his wife!
His wife! do you hear?—Did you dare? Had I spurned
Your love?—Yet I loved you . . . coward!"—A knife,

As she wheeled and caught at a cabinet—
A fang of scintillant steel, keen, cold—
Fell savagely twinkling; some curio met
Among Asian antiques bronze and gold,
Mystical, curiously graven and set.

"My Bactrian dagger! the prick of which
Through its ancient poison is death! . . . If so—
If you think you must love me—then " . . . and rich
Was the speech of her eyes in their poignant glow,
And my soul met hers at its passionate pitch.

And I whispered "Yes," for my brain had thought
A wild thought through—"why, life were a hell
To us so asunder!" And the blade I caught
With no nervous hand and she leaned and—well,
I stabbed her throat in its hollow, so naught

Might dabble its beauty. She tottered there
To a carven chair. I studied the blade
With its white-gold handle thick with the glare
Of devils in jewels, wildly inlaid;
Then my breast to the poisonous point rent bare.

One stain of blood on her throat and one
Dark red on my heart. And I held her and stood
Where a buhl clock ticked; and the sinking sun
Through the dull, sad eve burst banked with blood
And fell—One moment and all were done.

"When the young Earl comes," she whispered, "He—
He will leave us together. How deep the night!—
Do you hear the dance and the revelry?"
"Yes; and your checks are wet and white,
So cold! so cold! Valora, to me."

THE SUCCUBA.

I HAVE dreams where I believe
   I am prince of some dim palace;
One at morn my Genevieve
   Is at night the Lady Alice
Long, long dead, who was my bride;
And she glowers at my side
   Paly as a crystal chalice
Filled with fire diamond-dyed.

I have dreams and I shall die
   Wondering on them. I remember
In my sleep her icy eye
   Draws me with its mournful ember
Up a castle's stairs that pave
Alabaster to the wave,
   Ghostly in the gray November,
And my soul is all her slave.

Walls of darkness and of night
  Slit with casements tall of fire,
Ruby or a glowing white:
  As the wind breathes lower, higher,
Round the towers spirit things
Whisper, and a moaning sings
  In the strings of each huge lyre
Set upon its four chief wings.

In its corridors at tryst
  Flame-eyed phantoms meet. Its sparry
Halls are misty amethyst,
  Battlemented 'neath the starry
Dome of death that none has known;
Heavens with the green stars sown
  Low and large, and all their barry
Beams blown on an ocean lone.

Can it be a witch is she
  Or a vampire, who is whiter
Than the spirits of the sea?
  For my dreams inform her brighter

Than the faint foam-blossoms. Lo,
All this passion is my foe!
    For her love lies tighter, tighter
On my heart than utter woe.

I but vaguely know I live
    Two pale lives of sweetest sorrow,
Where my love must give and give
    Passion, that its soul must borrow
Of the living, to the dead,
To the dear unhallowéd;
    And should I be death's to-morrow,
If I knew I could not dread.

Lo, my dreams have drowned that place
    In all moon-white flowers: lilies
Like the influence of a face;
    Knots of pearly amaryllis;
Cactus-bulks with pulpy blooms
Puffy in the silver glooms;
    White each hill with daffadillies
O'er the olive ocean looms.

THE SUCCUBA.

But to me their fragrance seems
   Poison; and their lambent luster,
Spun of twilight and of dreams,
   Poison; and each frosty cluster
Hides a serpent's fang. And I,
Longing at an oriel high,
   In my soul make ache to muster
Heart to breathe of them and die.

Then I feel big eyes as bright
   As the sea-stars. Gray with glitter
Swims unto me, wound with light,
   She. Deep hangings sway and flitter
Loves and deeds of Amadis
Darkly worked. And lo, this is
   She the night brings, sweet and bitter,
With a bliss that is not bliss.

Still I kiss her eyes and hair;
   Smooth her tresses till their golden
Glimmer sparkles. Everywhere
   Shapes of strange aromas, holden

Of her halls, about us troop
Foggy forms, that float and stoop
  On slow swells of rolling, olden
Music odorous loop in loop.

Yet I see beneath it all,—
  All this sorcery,—a devil,
Beautiful and grandly tall,
  Broods with shadowy eyes of evil.
And I know, each lilac morn,
In that land a cactus-thorn,
  Monstrous on some lonely level,
Blooms for her I may not scorn.

I have dreams where I believe
  I am prince of some dim palace;
One at morn my Genevieve
  Is at night the Lady Alice
Long, long dead.—Who may be brave
Held and haunted of the grave?
  When through some unholy malice
One a prince is and a slave.

HIS FIRST MISTRESS.

REIGN OF LOUIS XIV.

THRICE on the lips and twice on the eyes
   I kiss you or ever I kiss your bosom—
When love is true would you have it wise,
Wise as the world goes? No; 'tis a blossom
Lovely and wise since it's lovely; content
To live or to die as its folly pleases:
Life is a rose and the rose's scent—
Love, that's born with the rose—nor ceases.

If I tell you the Marquis will die, will you smile?
And laugh when he's dead?—This powder, my lily,
That shows like an innocent sweet in the phial—
Do not touch it! breathe distant!—a poison Exili
Used a life to discover. Its formula left

To a pupil, (well worthy the master!) the prudent
And pious Sainte Croix. Him, of teacher bereft,
The devil, I deem, must have taken as student.

Quite a dealer in death. And ours was a case
That those difficult drugs of his laboratory
Demanded. I visited; found him; his face
Bent over a sublimate, safe from the hoary
Light particles, masked with a mask of fine glass.
I told him your danger, Marie, and expounded
Our passion, despair, with many an "alas!"
He smiled while a paste in a mortar he pounded.

Three fistfuls of Louis—he'd do it, he said:
A delicate dust, gum, liquid and metal
Crushed, crucibled—"Stay! tie this mask on your
 head;
You see, but a grain on this fuchsia's petal
Has shriveled and blasted it—look how it dries.
A perilous pulver . . . could Satan make better? . . .
To mix with that present of perfumes—she dies,
And who is the wiser? Or, say, in a letter

"To the husband of her who has smiled on you since
Another grows bald?"—And he poured in a bottle
The subtlty.—"Bah! be he beggar or prince,
If he kiss but the seal the venom will throttle."
"Well," I thought, "I will test ere I risk." Slyly drew
My stilleto; approached to the bandlet, that tightly
Supported his mask, its keen point—it was true:
Where it cracked he fell dead—he but breathed of it lightly.

Your letter is sealed and is sent. You are mine.
By now he has broken the wax . . . If there flutters
Some dust in his nostrils, yes, who will divine
That this has assassined? Our alchemist utters
No word!—you are happy? and I?—oh, I feel
That I love and am loved.—The tidings comes heavy
To-night to the King; you are there; you will reel—
Will faint!—Now away to the royal levee.

BEFORE THE BALL.

AS to my soul—'t is a pathos of passion;
As to my life—has a flavor of sin.
What would you have when such is the fashion
Was and will be of the world we are in?
Yes, I have loved—and have you? have you reckoned
The cost of a love?—I can tell you: as much
As a soul—Mine, a woman's: I learned it that second
I knew that I loved, and to death mine were such.

And his love? but dissembled that ardor's pure beauty.
I endured undeceived nor pretended; and gave
All that the wisdom demanded—my duty,
For I loved. And the world—why, I was his slave,—
Should it worry I pleased him? Propriety sorrowed,
Uprolling her eyes as occasion; she—well,
A lie overglossed with a modesty borrowed.
And I was but woman, the end was—I fell.

Through love? No; the woman; that visible woman
Men usually know. Heart knows how we know
Of its innermore beauty, the luminous human
Distinction that's character!—Look at the glow
Of the moon that is new; 'tis the slenderest sickle
Of ray. So the flesh gleams the feeblest line
Of light, that's the soul; should the sun of Love
    prickle,
Mark, the whole glory of woman divine.

Yes, I know how it is. I have glimmered my season
Prolonged of suffusion. You think it is strange
That I let you, say—love me? but why not? my reason
Requires illusions. They give me that change
Which quiets remembrance. You kiss me, I wonder;
When you say, "You are beautiful," well, am I glad
If I laugh? you declaim on my form," How no blunder
Of nature discords," if I sigh am I sad?

How you stare at my eyes! and my lips—must they
    languish
For kisses to redden? My eyes must be bright
As this jewel I drown in my hair, with its anguish

BEFORE THE BALL.

Of tortuous fire that quivers, to-night.
Tears? may be.—This showy? that silly white flower
Were lovelier? for me its simplicity—no!
The gem I prefer to th' exotic. The hour
Has struck: I am ready: my fan: let us go.

MASKS.

Cucullus non facit monachum.

GIVE it down as you have spoken
You could live it ere you knew
What love was—"a bauble broken
Foolish of a thing untrue."—
You,-Viola, with your beauty
Cloistered die a nun! No; you—
You must live, and 't is your duty.

There's your poniard; for the second
In this tazza dropped; the blood
On it scarcely hard. I reckoned
Happily that hour we stood
There beside your palace stairway,
Cowled with my Franciscan hood,
When I said there was a bare way.

MASKS.

In the transept there I found it—
Your revenge. I saw him wild
Stalking to the church; around it
Dogged him marking how he smiled
In the moonlight where he waited.
When the great clock beating dialed
Ten, I knew he would be mated.

Heaven or the deed's own devil!—
Hardly had his sword and plume
Vanished in the dusk, than, level
On the long lagune, did loom
Into moonlight-woven arches
Her slim gondola; all gloom;
One swart gondolier; no torches.

—Shadowy gondolas kept bringing
Revellers; and far the night
Rang with merriment and singing.—
From the imbricated light
Of the oar-vibrating water,
Gliding up the stairway, white,
Velvet-masked—the count's own daughter.

Quickly met her: whispered, "Flora,
Gaston.—*Mia*, till they go
One brief moment here, Siora.
She'll perceive us; she below
With the duchess diamonds sparkling
Round the inviolable glow
Of her throat—Must pass us darkling;

"'T is Viola!"—And I drew her
In the old neglected pile—
Under her close mask I knew her,
By the chin, the lips, the smile.
Through the marble-foliated
Window fell the moonrays. While
All the maskers passed we waited.

I had drawn the dagger. Turning
Called her by her name. Some lie
Of a passion sighed; her burning
Cheek on mine when, wavering by,
In the flare *his* form bejeweled
Gleamed. My very blood burned dry
With the hate his-presence fueled.

My revenge: Up-pushing slightly
Cowl, the mask fell and revealed
Balka as the poniard whitely
Flashed. The hollow dark re-pealed
One long shriek but once repeated.
Yet, I stabbed her thrice. She reeled
Dead. I thought of you. The heated

Horror on my hands, I tarried
Like the silence. Drawn aside
On her face the mask hung married
To her camphor-pallor. Wide
Eyes with terror—stone. One second
I regretted, then defied
All remorse. Your beauty beckoned,

And I left her. You had pointed
Me this way. I walked the way
Clear-eyed and . . . it has anointed
Us fast lovers? will you say
Yes? or for no love go nun it?
Let this cowled love grow gray?--
Learn to hate him, you've begun it.

HAUNTED.

I

WITHOUT a moon when night comes on
   There is a sighing in its trees
As of sad lips that no one sees;
And the strange forest dwindling, large
Beyond fenced fields, seems shadowy drawn
Into its shadows. Faint and wan
By the westeriaed portico
Stealing I go;
Through gardens where the weeds are rank;
Where, here and there in patch and bank,
Rise clumped close spiarees whose blooms
Seem dots of starlight; and the four
Syringas sweet heap, powdered o'er,
Thin flower-beakers of perfumes;
   And the dead flowering-almond tree

HAUNTED. 139

Once maiden-pink. Still bower on bower
The roses climb in blushing flower—
And from the roses shall I see
Her sad, sad eyes shine like the flowers
That nestle dew-drops hours on hours,
Wistful, as if reproaching me?

II

When midnight comes it brings a moon:
A scent is strewn
Of honey and wild-thorns broadcast
Beneath the stars. When I have passed
Under dark cedars, darker pines,
To beds of red petunias,
Cornflower and blue columbine;
Azaleas mauve half-choked with grass,
Wide peonies like wisps of shine;
'Neath cloying honey-suckle vines,
Piled deep and trammeled with the gourd
And morning-glory; drained the hoard
Of rich aroma; oft have heard
The plaintive note of some lost bird
Trickle through night, awakened where,

'Neath its thick lair of twisted twigs,
The jarring and incessant grigs
Hummed. Scent-drugged so, the tepid air
Made all my soul as heavy as
Dew-poppied grass.

III

And when the moon rose flushed and full,—
Like some sea-seen hesperian pool,
A splash of gold through tangling trees,—
There came slow sighings in the trees
As of sad lips that no one sees.
And when all in a mystic space
Her orb swam, amiable white,
Right in yon shattered casement high,
Made of a whisper and a sigh
I thought *her* face
Formed in a mist of tears; so slight,
So beautiful, its pensive grace
Was like an olden melody.

IV

I know long-angled on its floors,
Where windows greet the anxious East,

HAUNTED.

The moonshine pours
White squares of glitter and, at least,
Gives glimmer to its moaning halls:
Sleep-tapestried, dim corridores
Wake whispers; by its wasted walls
Stand shadows; and where streaked dusts lay
Their undisturbed, deep gray,
Walk vision-footed. I below
Hear the wind's sighings come and go
Through one great buckeye near her room.—
Ah! know I not how those broad flues
Of her old home the winds make hoarse?
Their deep throats growl and boom
With wafts that slink through avenues
Of summer, singing in their course
Where blossoms drip, to swing them back.
Oh! how I fear it! and the crack
Dry, warping stairs give; and the black
That drapes each room the mind informs
To fling from closets phantom arms! . . .

V

I see her face beseeching pressed
To the ruged, oaken floor; distressed,
Pinched in her blind and praying hands;

So desolate with anguish! wrenched
With all remorse mind understands:
Weak, writhen; still I scoffed and fled
So unrelenting! when again
Back soul-forgiving stole, fast-clenched
In staring eyes all the hard pain,
Cramped to dilation, with a groan
Found—huddled hush—as stone as stone,
Her white and dead! . . .

VI

Yes, there is moan
In all its crannies and lean shades
Make melancholy rooms where braids
The lacy moonlight. Slow have flown
The years! the years! and I have known
An anguish and remorse far worse
Than usual life's, and live, it seems,
Because to live is but a curse. . . .

VII

There lies their burying-place; that ground
Arched o'er with rusty iron; stone,

Mossy, squares in a spot for dreams.
Wild just the same; its roses waste
Limp, placid petals; and here some
Lie loose like puffs of foam
On bold unhealthy weeds; displaced,
Strew wiltings here my feet around.
Mad roses and mad thorns. Here moan
In Autumn noons gray wood-doves, and
The sad days slumber bland.

UNDER THE GREENWOOD TREE.

HOW I love you! do you know
   That my love anticipated,
     Years ago, your love and waited
Fearful of no No? . . .

Dry with heat and hot with hay,
   Where yon strip of daisied hollow
     Shady, circling beeches follow
Shall we wile away

What half hours the daylight hath?—
   See, the hardy harvest makers
     Straighten, reapers red and rakers,
O'er the last mown swath.

Like a gold flower falls the sun;
   Tenuous brightness all the heaven
     By the subtle weaver, Even,
One rich weft is spun . . . .

Why, I loved you from the time—
  You remember, do you not?—
  It was in your orchard-plot,
I was reading rhyme—

No! but reading; and 't was thus:
  "By the blue Trinacrian sea,
  Far in pastoral Sicily
With Theocritus,"

When you asked I told you that
  Awkwardly; for you had found
  Me long-lounged upon the ground
Drowsily a-chat

With the sage—Boccaccio.
  And I thought Lauretta grew
  Tall before me; and when you
Came upon me so,

Thought it was she: so the book
  Old Decameron in calf,
  In the weeds tossed with a laugh,
And arose to look

In Lauretta's eyes and thus—
    Found them yours. Well, was I red,
    When the tome's name asked, I said,
"It?—Theocritus."

You had come for cherries; these
    Ardently I climbed for while
    You encouraged with a smile
Me who sought to please.

Ah, love, two short years agone!—
    I shall ne'er forget how you
    In that dainty dress of blue
Muslin—No?—A lawn?—

While my hand unsparingly
    In your apron's sag, red-stained,
    Rich the juicy ripeness rained,
Looked beneath that tree.

And I asked you—for, you know,
    To my eyes those serious eyes
    Held such true philosophies!—
If you'd read Rousseau.

"His Confessions?"—"No."—"A chance
    Somewhat similar in June,
    At the castle quaint of Toune,
Over there in France,

"Him befell and"—well, was it
    Gallant then, you higher dressed,
    Dropping cherries on your breast
To indulge his wit?

May I kiss those lips that glow?—
    Look, the golden gleam has narrowed
    To one rent of rose, deep-arrowed
Yonder—let us go.

REVISITED.

I

UPLIFTED darkness and the owl-light breaks,
  Scuds the wild land pursuing patch with patch,
As when deep camomile a swift wind shakes.
How clumsily I raised the crazy latch! . . .
So.—When yon black bulk, light-absorbing, rakes
Again the moon's bald disk—
Out; and the storm may snatch
Again wet hair pulled lank with wind and rain
Two hours since.—There sweeps the beams again
A dark cloud-besom from the ragged plain . . .
Now! . . . Soul, be thine the risk! . . .

II

Close to the fellside hugs the bramble hollow
Whining with wind, a pausing wind that grieves

Through the one crippled ash, whose nervous leaves,
Sleep-worried, rattle wooden as the lips
Of dead men kissing. There a gnarled vine slips
Up a humped, cloven rock, that seems to wallow
A gorgon head of ugly writhings; heaves
When, heaped abruptly on it, *flare!*
Burst rain and tempest-glare.—
This fled, I follow
A thorny slip of path until
Is passed the storm-scarred hill.

III

Shall I not then be breathless, sinking sense,
For ghastlier yet to come?—No! sterner strength
Is in my soul!—Beyond the hill the dense,
Dead wood remains and then—that livid length
Of mooning waters spectral and immense
With sullen storm and night.
There, if the ghoulish wind—
Which knows well as I know how I have sinned;
—Will cease to curse me, wakeful in its spite,
Disturbed with horror only of my soul,
I'll find among cramped reeds, the storm has thinned,

His wide white eyes, metallic in the light
Of the impassive moon: In gusty roll
Of washing ripples, webby, slippery locks
Dabbling and dead: Or wedged among sharp rocks,
Wild-pinched and water-strangled white,
His faded face that mocks.

LOST LOVE.

I LOVED her madly. For—so wrought
    Young Love divining isles of Truth
    Large in the central seas of Youth—
"Love will be loved," I thought.

Once when I brought a rare wild-pink
    To place among her plants, the wise,
    Still guerdon of her speaking eyes
Said more than thanks, I think.

Oh, you frail Marguerita! oh,
    Weak woman in the woman! You
    Speak! can such hearts be all but true
To hearts that love them so!

She loved another. Ah! too well
    I have the story in my soul!—
    A weary tale the weary whole
Of how she loved and fell.

LOST LOVE.

I loved her so! . . . Remembering of
    My mad grief then, I wonder why
    It is such griefs grow dull and die
While lives still live and love.

Strange, is it not? For grief was dear
    To me as she once. A regret
    It is now; just to make eyes wet
And lift a big lump here.

Yet, had she lived as dead in shame
    As now in death, love would have used
    Pride's pitying pencil and abused
The memory of her name.

This makes me thank my God, who led
    My broken life in sunlight of
    This pure affection, that my love
Lives by her being dead.

LYANNA.

THE Summer came over the southern ocean,
    Girdled with fire, tiaraed with light;
Laughter her eyes and her lips a potion
    To quaff, to kindle, and know its might;
A shadow that sparkled and flashed; a motion
    Blushed from the uttermost South, and I,
Of the race of the Sylphs, far over the ocean
    Followed her up the sky.

An exile aye to the mists that muster,
    Pulsing with pearl and braided with blue,
Large, luminous ghosts in the hazy bluster
    Low of the winds, where my brother-crew,

When the day dreams up, in their bright bands cluster,
    Ranges of glitter through cloudy gold,
At the gates of the Dawn, whose limbs are lustre,
    To wait till her gates unfold.

And the Summer murmured me "Follow! follow!"
    Whispered and promising whispered, "Love!"—
Winged with the wings of the sweeping swallow
    Followed I wings of the drifting dove:
"Love, and a mortal," and fain would I follow;
    "Love, and immortal," my flight was strong;
"Life!" and my life seemed vain and hollow;
    "Love!" and my heart was song.

Fleet as the winds are fleet, yea, and fleeter
    Far than the stars, that throbbed like foam
Through the billowy blue, in musical meter
    Winnowed our wings; and the golden gloam
Rang; and life was a passion completer
    Than Edens of flowers; and faith a lyre
That sang at the heart to make hope sweeter,
    And hope, a leaping fire.

So to the North our wings went maying
    Resonant ways, till a castle shone
Gaunt on great cliffs, and the late skies graying
    O'er walls of war and its towers lone.
A fall of steps to the sea where spraying
    Thundered the breakers; and terrace and stair,
Rock o'er the waters, rose rosy and raying
    Deep in the sunset glare.

A dew drop burns when the dawn lights prickle;
    All of my being tingled to light,
Blossomed against her tarrying fickle,
    White on the terraced height.
Beauty that stood like a moon in sickle,
    A slender moon that the winds bleach bleak,
With its hue like honeys that drop and trickle
    From combs whose wax is weak.

In dreams I came to her, lo! as a vision:
    Yea, in her sleep as a dream was wound:
Of her vestal chastity held: a prison
    Her innermost spirit that took and bound.

And her rest I stole, for sleep in derision
   Mocked at my hope for a love that slept:
And her soul I awakened. Lo! it had risen
      And answered my soul and wept.

"Lyanna, I hoop thee with arms of fire!"—
   My words like kisses were sparks that smote,—
"Lyanna, my life is a single wire,
   Thy love is its single note.
Hast thou known me thus? Shall it sound entire,
   Full as the angels' who hover and harp
To the glory that's God, like one silver lyre
      Borne in a beam that is sharp? . . .

"Gladdened a splendor of rose, a splendor
   Out of the East and the ruby bloom
Hiding—what, love? Two eyes that are tender?
   Two lips that are sweet, and limbs of perfume
And fragrant fire? And who was the sender
   To thee of this lover?" And bending low
Honeyed my speech as a flower's that, slender,
      Buds when the wild stars blow.

LYANNA.

Seemed all her passionate pulses to quicken;
  Flowed all her soul to her eyes; but Sleep
Trembled her voice so it seemed to thicken
  With a love that was sighing to weep:—
"Yea, I divined thee, yea, and was stricken;
  Light was thy messenger-dove of love.
Alas! I divined, and I seemed to sicken,
  To perish and pine thereof.

"White are the clouds, but I knew thee whiter
  Than dazzling domes of the Dawn, I knew;
Bright are God's stars, but thine eyes were brighter,
  Brighter and burning blue.
And my love was thine, though it held thee slighter
  Than breezes bruiting it murmuring by;
And waited and yearned and the yearning tighter
  Than tears in the hearts that die.

"'Lyanna! Lyanna!' thou calledst ever:
  'Lyanna!' A ripple of rays that came:
'Lyanna, thy name is like light forever!'
  And I marveled at my name.

For the word was such as if stars should sever
   To an utterance slow of syllabled beams;
'Lyanna! Lyanna!' I turned, but never
         Informed thee more than my dreams.

"Thou walkedst a beauty afar; a glitter
   Of gleaming aroma; and I amoan
Flung thee mine arms; and thy gaze was bitter
   Was calmer and sterner than stone;
Avoiding thou passedst in scorn. Oh, fitter
   The hate of all heaven to me than this!
Yea, scorn!—and I wept, when oh! a flitter
         Of fire, a laugh, and a kiss." . . .

So I won her then. And the lungs of the thunder
   Trumpeted tempest; and dark the seas
Lunged at the walls like a roaring wonder,
   And the black rain buzzed like bees.
"Lyanna, my bride!" And the heavens asunder
   Rushed—chasms of glaring storm where ran
The thunder's cataracts rolling under—
         For, behold, her race was man.

LYANNA.

Mine, of the elements. At the moth-white portal
  Of dreams stood the soul with her name. I saw
Lyanna and said, "Of the utterly mortal
  Mine the eternal lot and law!—
Thou lovest me?"—"Oh! and I love thee!"—"Immortal
  Is mine through thy love,—for thou lovest!"—'T is
    said,
Behold! when they came in the morn, a-startle
      Were lips with, " Lyanna is dead!"

GLORAMONE.

THE moonbeams on the hollies glow
  Pale where she left me; and the snow
Lies bleak as moonshine on the graves,
Ribbed with each gust that shakes and waves
Ancestral cedars by her tomb.

She was more beautiful for death
In death's dim loveliness. The gloom,
The iciness that takes the breath,
The sense of worms, were not too strong
To keep me from beholding long.

I stole into the mystery of
Her old, armorial tomb; and Love
Sighed all its romance in my heart:

Soft indistinctness of pale lips
Breathed on my hair; faint finger tips
Fluttered their starlight on my brow;
Vague kisses on my eyes and now,
Hard on my lips, an aching sense
Of vampire winning. And I heard
Her name slow-syllabled—a word
Of haunting harmony—and then
Low-throated, "Thou! at last, 't is thou!"
And far off shadowy sighs again.

How madly strange that this should be!
For, had she loved me when of earth,
It were not now so marvelous,
So marvelous remembering me
With dead for living love, though worth
Less, yes, far less to both of us.
And long I wondered listening there,
"What deed of mine or thought hath wrought
This love from hate in after-life
She giveth back?" and everywhere
Around my life I thought and thought
And—nothing; only, how my love

Had still persisted for her hate
That made her Appolonio's wife.
Her hate! her lovely hate!—for of
Her naught I found unlovely—and
I felt she did not understand
My passion, so 't were well to wait.

And now I knew her presence near,
I full in life; yet had no fear
. There in the sombre silence, mark.
And it was dark, yes, deathful dark:
But when I slowly drew away
The pall, death modeled with her face,—
From face and limbs it fell and lay
Rich in the dust,—the shrouded place
Was glittering daggered by the spark
Of one rare ruby at her throat,
Red-hearted with star-arrowy throbs
That made it pulse. And note on note
The blackness fought with finest sobs
Of glimmering as of that stone.
Lustrous and large against her throat
As her large eyes when they could see.

And standing by her corpse alone
I doubted not her loving me.

Red essence of an hundred stars
In fretful crimson through and through
Its bezels beat, when, bending down,
My hot lips kissed her heart. And scars
Of veiny scarlet and of blue,
Flame-hearted, blurred the midnight and
The vault rang; and I felt her hand
Like fire in mine. And, lo, a frown
Broke up her face as gently as
A breeze that jolts the graining grass
And spills its rain-drops. When this passed,
Through song-soft slumber binding fast,
Slow smiles dreamed outward beautiful,
And with each smile I heard the dull
Deep music of her heart and saw,
As by some necromantic law,
Faint tremblings of a lubric light
Float through white temples and white throat;
And each long pulse was as a note,
That gathering, like a strong surprise

With all its happiness, again
Left her arch lips one wistful smile
That lingered languidly. Yet pain
Slept 'neath her eyelids, wasted white,
Insufferable. . . . Did those eyes
Grow wide unto my kisses?—Yea,
They were unsealed! And all the fire
Of that dark ruby at her throat,
Arrow by arrow, in them smote;
And as some harmony entire
Was she, but how, I can not say.

And forth into the night I brought
Her beautiful, and o'er the snow,
Where moonbeams on the hollies glow,
I led her. And her feet no print,
No lightest trace in frost, no dint
Left of their nakedness. I thought,
"The moonlight fills them with its glow
And covers; and the tomb was black,
Then this strong light—yes!" turning back
My eyes met hers; and as I turned,
Flashing centupled facets, burned

That red gem at her throat; and I
Pondered its ardor for a while:
How came it there, and when, and why?
Who set it at her throat? again,
Why was it there? So studying
I questioned. And a far, strange smile
Filled all her face, and secret pain
Gave to her words a bitter ring:
"Thou! thou! alas!" she said and sighed;
"And if I am not dead, 't was thou!
Canst thou remember of it now?"
"Yes." And she leaned unto me, eyed
Like some wise serpent that hath still
Lain all night on wild rocks to stare
At amaranthine stars until
Its eyes have learned their glassy glare.

And then I took her by the wrists
And drew her to me. Faintly felt
The sorrow of her hair, whose mists
Fell twilight-deep and dimly smelt
Still of the worm and tomb. And she
Smiled on me with such sorcery

As well might win a soul from God
To fiends and furies. And I trod
On white enchantments and was long
A song and harp-string to a song,
Love's battle in my blood. And there,
Kissing her throat, her mouth, her hair,
I stole the jewel from her throat
With crafty fingers, to admire
The witchcraft of its fevered fire.
It in the hollow of my hand
A rosy spasm seemed to float
Red, red with anger: then a brand
Touched scorching, and I felt it run
Swift in my pulses like a sun
Of torrid poison. And I marked
My palm brim full with blood; a-glow
Big drops globed beadings, oozing slow,
Like holly-berries, on the snow.
Then all the night contracting darked
Upon me and I heard a sigh,
So like a moan, 't was as if years
Of anguish bore it; and the sky
Swam near me as when seen through tears.

And she was gone. In ghostly gloom
Of swart, scarred pines a crumbling tomb
Loomed like a mist. Carved in its stone,
Above the grated portal deep,
Glimmered the legend of her sleep,
"*Death crowned with Death one, Gloramone.*"

THE CAVERNS OF KAF.

[LOVE SENSUAL.]

ONE Benreddin, I have heard,
    Near the town of Mosul sleeping,
In a dream beheld a bird
    Wonderful with plumes of sweeping
Azure crowned pomegranate-red.
Seeming near him, while it fled
Brilliant as a blossom, peeping
Down the Tigris him it led.

Following, the creature came
    To a haggard valley, shouldered
Under peaks that had no name,
    Where it vanished: on the bouldered

Savageness a woman fair
In a white simarre rose there,
Beckoning; around her smouldered
Pensive lights of purple air.

Then he found himself in vast
 Caves of sardonyx, whose ceiling
Domed one chrysoberyl. Blast
 In blast of music, stealing
From an aural glory, nears;
Waxing on his eager ears,
Far recedes in clashes pealing
Psalteries and dulcimers.

Wildly sculptured walls did heave
 Slabs of story, where, embattled,
Warred Amshaspand and the Deev;
 Over all two splendors rattled
Arms of heaven, arms of hell;
Forms of flame that seemed to swell
Godlike: Aherman who battled
With Ormuzd he might not quell.

And Benreddin wondered till
  The reverberant rapture drifting,
Strong beyond his utmost will,
  Rolled him onward where, high lifting
Pillar and entablature,
Vast with emblem, yawned a door—
Valves of liquid lightning shifting
In and out and up and o'er . . .

Walls of serpentine deep-domed
  Gray with agate and with beryl;
Tortuous diaper crusted foamed
  Rough with jewels; and as peril
Difficult a colonnade
Ran of satin-spar to fade
Far in labyrinths of sterile
Tiger-eye that twisting grayed.

Dizzy stones of magic price
  Crammed volute and loaded corbel;
Iridescent shafts of ice
  Leapt: with long reëchoed warble

THE CAVERNS OF KAF. 171

Waters unto waters sang;
Curling arc and column sprang
Into fire as each marble
Fountain flung its drift that rang.

And against him, filled with sound,
   Surfs of resonant colors jetted;
Sun-circumferences that wound
   Out of arcades crescent-fretted,
Mists of citron and of roon,
Lemon lights that mocked the moon,
Shot with scarlet veined and netted,
Beating golden hearts of tune.

Discs of rose-nasturtium;
   Orbs of down-dilating splendor;
In whose cores did slowly come
   Spots like serpent eyes that slender
Glared with undecided beams;
Panting through dissolving gleams
Hissings of clear fire tender
As an houri's breath who dreams.

Characters of Arabic,
   Cabalistic, red as coral,
Through vague violet veils did prick
   Changing; as if fierce at quarrel
Iran wrote of Turan there
Hate and scorn, or everywhere
Wrought swift talisman and moral
Stern the Afrits might not dare.

Sunset splendors drew him on
   To a cavern's crystal hollow,
Hewn of alabaster wan,
   Lucid, whence his gaze could follow
Far transparent flights in flights
Rolling, drowned in sounding lights
Glaucous gold; he like some swallow
O'er a lake the morning smites.

Curved the vault mosaiced in
   With the sensuous limbs of Peries:
Restless eyes of Deevs and Jinn
   In the walls watched. Unseen faeries

From the dim dome rained and tossed
Flowers of fire full of frost,
Flowers of frost a fire that carries
Smoldering an incense lost.

Through the air, in groups of grace,
  Naked odalisques of heaven
Of Arabian gold did lace
  Flaming censers, spouting seven
Jets of burning perfume green;
To each globe of garnet, seen
As it swung, new form was given
Hippogrif or rosmarine.

Aloes, nard and ambergris;
  Saffron, cinnamon and civet;
All aromas strange that kiss
  Sense with scent and hold and rivet
Soul to soul,—that have grown dull
With life's lassitude,—to lull,
These with amorous hands did give it,
Vaporous and beautiful.

And Benreddin's passive soul,
　　To hot eyes intoxicated,
Ached. And sucking at the whole
　　Nipple of flushed Pleasure, sated
Sucked unsatisfied. It saw
Cheeks of light without a flaw;
Breasts of bloom with breathings bated;
Limbs translucent nearer draw.

Houri eyes and wafted hair
　　Brilliant blackness. Then a thunder
Of hoarse music, that did bear
　　Upward, organed in the under
Caverns of the demon world.
Koran scrolls in glisten curled
Sparkling by him; and a wonder
Of cœrulean mottoes swirled.

Then one long note made of sighs,—
　　A muezzin cry repeated
Dying downward,—filled with eyes,—
　　Melting from him,—passion-heated;

Saddening into sounds of spray
Choral. Then one rocking ray
Angry burned and angry fleeted
From intensest blood to gray. . . .

And, 't is told, this life was young,
   Young that sun-dawn. When the darting,
Anguish-throated bulbuls sung,
   Through the silent starlight starting,
One, a Baghdad merchant, led
By the white light on its head,
Found a hoary shadow. Parting
Hair from face, Benreddin—dead.

THE SPIRIT OF THE VAN.

[LOVE IDEAL.]

MIDSUMMER-NIGHT; the Van; through night's
    wan noon,
Wading the storm-scud of an eve of storm,
Pale o'er Carmarthen's peaks the mounting moon.
    Hills of Carmarthen! sullen heights that swarm
Girdling lone waters as gaunt wizards might
    Crouch guarding some enchanted gem of charm—
Hills of Carmarthen, that for me each night
    Reëcho prayers and pleadings one long year
Unanswered, made to listening waters white!—
    The bitter blue of Winter, and the clear
Calm eyes of girlish Springtide, and the slow
    Brown gaze of languid Summer, and the cheer,
Bleak-eyed, of tristful Autumn saw me so,
    Unhappy, lost among the hollow hills.

Should any ripple tremble into glow,
  When yeasty moonshine sprays the foam, there
    thrills
Heart's expectation through fleet veins and high
  "'T is she!" each pulse with exultation shrills.
But 't is not—never! Once ... and then would I
  Had lain abolished so beholding! . . . World,
What sadder hast than beauty that must die?—
  Drugged so with beauty, if some fiend had curled
Stiff talons through long hair, and twisting tight,
  Scoffed, "Burn and be!" launch into hell had hurled
Me satisfied to happiness—Love's white
  Bloom heavenizing hell—I, unamerced,
Shackled with tortures, well might mock hell's spite.
—Immortal memory of light, I thirst!
O shining star-stain to what being wove,
  In that I love thee am I so accursed?
Oh, make me mad with love, with all thy love!
  Who bruit it to these wilds when midnights gloom
Storms or drip gold the sibylline stars above;—
  When thy high favors all heaven's wealth consume,
Foil to thy potent presence,—and make mad
  Me with a madness sick as from perfume.

Sleep may I not now for soft sleep is sad.
    Cheated of thee, sad are all tearful dreams,
Haunted by shining sorrowings unclad.—
    Strange, tyrannous hope in life that only seems!
And seeming hope forever needs must pine
    Hugging this vanishment of form-fixed beams!—
Though thou be wrought from elements divine,
    And I crass earth exalted, which will think,
"Since I am thine this makes me hope thee mine,"
    Must I, its usual phantom, the still brink
Of thy lone lake bewilder nightly? Yearn·
Toward that vast vision of a moment's wink?
When, glassing out great circles, which did urn
    Some intense essence of interior light,—
As clouds that clothe the moon unbinding burn,
    Ruptured, stands forth her orb, triumphant white,—
Middle the Van churned foam like feathering fire,
    Dilating ivory. Expectant night
Tip-toed attentive, fearful to suspire;
    And there up-soared—what glittering majesty?
What goddess sensed with glory and desire?
    One instant's moiety whirled up to be—
Love! and sucked down where burst a brassy black

THE SPIRIT OF THE VAN.

O'er cloven waves that sighed for ecstacy.
In multifarious colors swallowed back—
  Pale pearl and lilac, asphodel and rose,
Tempestuous crocus curling crack in crack.

And I alone to marvel as who knows
He is not dead and yet it seems he is,
  Tranced but in body while the spirit glows.—
O world-sweet face! brow one wide angel kiss!
  High immortality!—to image such
Dance starlight in a lily's loveliness.—
  Waste-bound with moony gold, too gross to clutch
Such queening chastity, though clear as gum
  On almugs globed and fragrance to the touch:
And hair—not hair! lithe rays that seemed to come
  Strained through the bubble of a chrysolite,
Soft quiverings of light that clung and clomb.
  Such left me such; deep on my soul's quick sight
Eternal seared; my life—a stealing shade
  Scouting the day and ardent of the night:
A raver to the hoary hills which laid
  Their dumb society in ruth on who
Shunned all companionship of man and maid:

THE SPIRIT OF THE VAN.

Boon comrade of the mountain blossoms blue:
Instructed intimate of trees that they—
  Wise as the legendary world that drew
Oracles from lips in oaks—might, haply, say
  Prophetic precepts to me: how were won
A spirit loved to love an one of clay:
In vain.
       When one day, log-like in the sun
Beside his cave, where twisted mandrakes rank,
  Puce, hairy henbane coppery blossoms spun,
Wrinkled as Magic, I a grizzled, lank
  Squat something startled; naught save skin and hair;
With eyes wherein two demons brewed and drank
  Disputing dreams, which made them shrink or glare;
Familiars who, beholding me draw near,
  Croaked lips of famine, lean fangs grinning bare,
"Woo her with combs of running honey clear,
  And white loaves of a seven-times bolted wheat.
Climb to thy love and crawl! fear not and fear!"

  This have I done these many months. Repeat
Vows low-lipped sunk with passionate offering
  Of loaves o'erbolted, honey seven-times-sweet.

Still woe and woe is mine. Now I but bring
  My simple self to-night, ungifted, see;
Myself unto thee!—Shall this clay still cling
  Clogging fulfillment? thy love's mastery
Be balked by flesh? No!—plunge it deep and fly
  Down to thy mounted throne of majesty!
Gathering bright limbs one splendid instant—die
  To epochs o' th' elements! for one kiss
Forfeit this human immortality!
  Breathe with thy breathing waters, laugh and hiss
Where lion-tawnyness extending creeps
  Orb into disc there 'round thy templed bliss!
Dream, dream o'er wave-blue lazuli which heaps,
  Rude-hewn, rough, rugged turret, wall, and dome,
Thy glaucous chambers where the green day sleeps!
  Dead not with death!—
                  What secrets hath thy home
Not mine then storied in exultant foam!—
Deeper, down deeper! mark me, yea, I come!

THE SPIRIT OF THE STAR.

[LOVE SPIRITUAL.]

THERE is love for love; the heaven
    Teems with possibilities;
Earth has such as heaven has given,
    Earth and all her sister seas.
Heaven and earth and sea is gladder
For it; only man is sadder,
Waxing wise in night for driven
    Drift of light he never sees.

There are lives for lives; and beauty
    Born for beauty; for your earth
Faith celestial given as booty
    To mortality of worth;

Song for every song; unfolding
Hope for dying hope; a holding
Duty towards aspiring duty
   Godly as the laws of birth.

Earth and ocean are prolific
   Of wild wonders as our sky;
With fine shapes of fair, terrific,
   Who, if loved, shall never die:
Dæmons rugged as their mountains;
Spirits sunny as their fountains;
Sylphids of the wind pacific
   As the stars they tremble by.

I was lonely; long had waited
   For the sweet eternal sleep;
Watching where the worlds dilated,
   Waned or wasted in the deep.
Where beneath my star a planet
Whirled and shone like glowing granite,
While around it swung and grated
   Orbs of fire sweep in sweep.

I was sad; the silence wilted
   On me like a scentless bud
Fading ere it blows. The quilted
   Clouds, like bursts of beating blood,
Streamed beneath me; and the starry
Still serene above bent barry,—
Thick with golden splashes tilted,—
   Seemed with arms of angels strewed.

I was loveless with a yearning
   After love that never came;
All my being's fineness burning
   Outward, to no blushing shame
Immolated; but a splendor
Of intention that was tender
To compulsion; all returning
   On my love with fiercer flame.

So I left the stars whose lances
   Shook their arrowy gold in heat
Of hard hyacinth; the glances
   Of their million moony feet

Ranged about me leaving. Beating
Downward, left them still repeating
Far farewells; the trembling trances
  Of their white eyes falling sweet.

Came unto your moon; vast alleys
  Of white jasper cleaving hills
Of chalcedony, whose valleys
  Cataracting crystal fills.
Twixt two mountains—like a vision
Seen through jewel-gates Elysian—
Growing as a music dallies
  Into forms of dreams it thrills,—

Long walls rose of beaming nacre
  Cloudy; coiling peace around
Acre upon arching acre
  Of a city without bound:
Caryatids alternated
With Atlantes sculpture-weighted;
And its gates—some god the maker—
  Leaves of symboled diamond.

In the pure light rocking, swimming
　　Domes of dazzle swirl on swirl,
Lifted columned temples brimming
　　Oval roofs of silver curl;
Galleries of spar that sparkled;
　　Pillared palaces that darkled
Moonstone, opal; and, far dimming,
　　Aqueducts of ghostly pearl.

Streaming steeples sharp of dædal·
　　Emblem, each an obelisk
Wrought of lividness, whose needle
　　Balanced bubble, crescent, disc;
Some of diamond, like a blister
Frozen; some of topaz, glister
Vinous; and each burning middle
　　Dazzled like the eyes of Risk.

Still I left it and descended
　　Worldward. For the longing drew
Me, and drawing me was blended
　　With your Earth I never knew.

THE SPIRIT OF THE STAR.

And did star and moon forsake me,
   I had answered what did take me
Worldward, where it lay a splendid
   Blossom in a sea of dew.

And when night came, lo, above you
   Sleeping by your folded sheep,
O'er the hills I rose; to love you
   Came, and kissed you in your sleep.
And the destinies had brought it
So I told you, you who thought it
Not so strange that I should love you,
   I a spirit of the deep.

Ah, you knew how she had found you
   Sometime in some life not sad;
Won your soul to hers and bound you
   With chaste kisses that were glad.
Days forget, but nights remember;
And my love shall live an ember
In you when the world around you
   Scoffs at this as one who's mad:

Idol Beauty! be one petal
  To its passion-flower! far
Past Earth's ignorance—a metal
  Rusting that reflects no star!—
Live beyond men lest they shame you!
Lest their shame, not I, should blame you!
Dream! and when the shadows settle,
  Be the dream you dream you are!

AT NINEVEH.

"I was that Syrian slave who loved a king
"Assyrian, with love that lived to hold
"No hope beyond the madness of the thing."

And she was beautiful as noons of gold;
   And amorous as nights that swoon their stars
O'er lands of romance. And the tale is told

How, clad with day, between ranked warriors
   Steel-lustrous, down the hall of audience,
'Mid pillared trophies of barbaric wars,

She came unto his throne and asked, "Lord, whence
   Is love and why?" He, musing on her, said:
"O slave, man's love lies with the gods and hence,

"Divine, is known but of the Spirithead.   [why,
    'Why?' dost thou question? there! we know not
Unless 't is love which makes us deathless dead."

Smiled; and the woman passioning each eye
    With all the love that stammered in her blood,
Dumb with wild language, clasped her hands on high,

And in her veiling hair knelt, sobbing: "Good,
    O king, thy answer! for, behold, I love!—
What freak of fate hath set this bitter brood,

"Urned dusts of kings, between this love, whereof
    The rubric reads, 'The ashes of your dead
Shall shriek dishonored,' yet I dare" . . . "Enough!"

He, motioning.   Then for a second fed
    His gaze along her faultless form and face,
Pointing cried, "Rhana! strike me off her head!"

A tall deep-chested slave with tawny grace
    Strode at the mandate from the press.   A form
Royally favored.   Deep a night-dark lace,

AT NINEVEH.

Her thick hair twisting to one supple arm,
   Flashed broad a blade the other. Rising shone
With light the swift death—fell; and dripping warm

Lifting the head he stood before the throne.
   And he who scowled there, "By the gods, 't is well!
When slaves begin to babble"—As hewn stone

Stern stood the slave, a son of Israel.
   Then striding on the monarch, in his eye
The wrath of heaven and the hate of hell,

Shrieked, "Lust! I loved her! look on us and die!"
   Swifter than fire clove him to the brain.
Kissing that head he held fell with the cry—

Loud in the fury of the stabbing rain
A thousand weapons thrust against him slain—
"Judge, God of Israel, between us twain!"

ROMAUNT OF THE OAK.

"I RIDE to death, for my love is shame—
The Lady Maurine of noble name,

"Whose love is a lie!—Though life be long
Is love the wiser?—Love made song

"Of all my life; and the soul, that crept
Before, arose like a star and leapt:

"Still leaps, though it holds love less than true,
Than noble, though pure as a spark of dew."

The crest of his foeman, a heart of white
In a bath of fire, burned the night.

The stranger knight rode on and sung.
His lance in the lover stuck and clung. . . .

What woman is this in the weary dawn
With the wildwood shadows standing wan?

Who kneels, one hand on her straining breast,
One hand on the dead man's bosom pressed?

Her face as dim as the dead's; as cold
As his tarnished armor of steel and gold?

She hales him under the olden oak,
Whose ruined trunk the wild-vines choke.

She stands him stiff, in his foreign arms,
In its hollow heart: "Be safe from storms,"

She laughs. And his cloven casque is placed
On his brow; and his riven shield is braced.

She sings, as she gathers the forest flowers,
"The dead have brides, and the dead are ours."

And stares and stares.—When the moon arose
Laughed, as it grew a full-blown rose,

"The wreath on my hair as the moon is fresh,
Eke the braid on his brow, on his neck the mesh.

"Ho, moon, shalt shrivel; wild roses gay,
Shall wilt; my heart, shalt wither away." . . .

Where the ghostly paths with the shade were dark
The wild roes stalked, and stood as stark

As phantoms with eyes of flame, or fled—
Like silence pursued—down the darkness dead.

And the night grew harsh with the tempest's cry.
In the oak with her warrior she would lie.

When she heard his harness rattle and groan
As the storm beat the oak and its boughs were blown,

She shrunk in sobbing, "He's calling me,
'Come, shelter thee from the fiends dost see.'

"He knows; for his eyes are balls of heat
Glowing the love of his heart's dead beat.

"Wilt thou make it warm—this living heart
With thy heart of dust?—Now who shall part?" . . .

They found her closed in his armored arms.—
Had he claimed his bride on that night of storms?

www.ingramcontent.com/pod-product-compliance
Lightning Source LLC
Chambersburg PA
CBHW020848160426
43192CB00007B/827